The Virtues
that build us up

The Virtues
that build us up
More Life Lessons From Great Literature

by

Mitchell Kalpakgian

A Crossroad Book
The Crossroad Publishing Company
New York

Acknowledgements

While many of these essays are new and unpublished, a number of them have appeared in earlier, shortened, differently edited versions. They are reprinted here with permission. I am most appreciative and grateful to the editors of these publications: Pieter Vree, *New Oxford Review*; Joseph Pearce, *Saint Austin Review*, Father David Meconi, S.J., *Homiletic and Pastoral Review*, and John Moorehouse, *Catholic Men's Quarterly*.

The following essays were published in *New Oxford Review*: Chapter 5 "The Wisdom of the World and the Wisdom of God" appeared as "The Wisdom of the World & the Wisdom of God (November 2009); Chapter 6 "The Virtues of the Heart: The Mark of Civilization" appeared as "Virtues of the Heart" (June 2010); Chapter 9 "The Treasures or Prizes of life" appeared as "The Great Rewards of Civilization" (April 2011); Chapter 10 "The Manliness of Chivalry" appeared as "Chivalry Scorned Is Love Denatured" (October 2000); Chapter 12 "St. Monica: Mother, Wife, and Homemaker as Saint" appeared as "St. Monica: Mother, Wife, & Homemaker as Saint (February 2002); Chapter 14 "The Empty Self versus the Rich Soul" appeared as "The Empty Self vs. the Rich Soul" (January 2004; Chapter 15 "The Inspiration of the Muses and the Power of Beauty" appeared as "To Live Well & Enjoy the Beauty of the Arts" (September 2016).

The following essays appeared in *Homiletic & Pastoral Review*: Chapter 2 "The Fullness of the Truth and the Sin of Sloth" (May 2003); Chapter 8 "Crucified Love and Martyrdom in Shakespeare's *King Lear*" (May 2009).

The following essays were published in *Saint Austin Review*: Chapter 1 "The Life of the Mind" appeared as "*Rasselas* and the Life of the Mind (March/April 2009); Chapter 7 "The Magic of Childhood Memories in Andersen's "Snow Queen" appeared with that same title (March/April 2011). Chapter 18 "*Motion and Rest in Frost's Poetry: Stopping, Pausing, Rushing, and Traveling*" appeared by the same title (May/June 2016).

One essay appeared in *The Catholic Men's Quarterly*: Chapter 3 "The Perennial Philosophy versus Ideology" (Summer/Fall 2006).

The Crossroad Publishing Company
www.crossroadpublishing.com

Crossroad, Herder & Herder, and the crossed C logo/colophon are trademarks of The Crossroad Publishing Company.

In continuation of our 200-year tradition of independent publishing, The Crossroad Publishing Company proudly offers a variety of books with strong, original voices and diverse perspectives. The viewpoints expressed in our books are not necessarily those of The Crossroad Publishing Company, any of its imprints, or of its employees. No claims are made or responsibility assumed for any health or other benefits.

Library of Congress Cataloging-in-Publication Data available from the Library of Congress.

ISBN: 978-0-8245-2075-5

Printed in the United States of America

Dedication

To all who formed my mind, shaped my education, and blessed me with the gift of their wisdom: In memory of Khatchig and Meline Kalpakgian, beloved parents with minimal education but with a profound knowledge from life experience, Armenian folk ways, and a Christian love of family; in memory Dr. Miriam Ryan, a high school Latin teacher in Milford, Massachusetts, with a passion for learning and a zeal for teaching who inspired a love of reading; in memory of professors Dennis Quinn and Franklyn Nelick of Kansas University who taught literature as living knowledge, a repository of the world's accumulated wisdom, and timeless universal truths that never age.

In memory of my wife Joyce, a dream come true, an answer to a prayer, a gift from heaven, and the fulfillment the heart's desire to love and be loved.

To my children and grandchildren, the abundant fruits of love and the copious harvest of life. "My cup runneth over."

Table of Contents

Chapter 1. The Life of the Mind

Just as Hippocrates taught that physical health depends upon food and exercise, wise men and great thinkers have said a similar thing about the life of the intellect: it requires certain foods of the mind in the right balance and proportion and vigorous mental exercises to achieve intellectual excellence. Medicine and education are known as "cooperative arts," that is, practices that depend on the person's desire for health and knowledge and the willingness to cooperate with the art of the knowledgeable physician or teacher to achieve health or excellence. Medicine and education are cooperative arts in another sense: the doctor depends upon nature to do the healing, and the teacher relies upon the reason of the student to discover the truth. The doctor does not really heal; nature does the healing. The teacher does not really teach; reason discovers the truth by using its natural power to know. The doctor and teacher, however, can prescribe the right food, exercise, and air—a proper course of action, a regimen or discipline—that will allow the body's natural capacity for healing and the mind's inherent power of knowing to act without the obstacles that prevent nature from performing its activity. Physicians determine the healthy condition of the body by drawing blood samples, measuring blood pressure, and requiring a stress test and by interpreting these vital signs. Traditional educators judge the status of the life of the mind according to criteria that measure a person's capacity to know and think. One of these criteria is the perennial ideal of Western education known as liberal arts: Does a person know how to read, write, speak, listen, and calculate? Does the person possess a mind "replete with images" to use the ideal of Dr. Johnson, the eminent man of letters of the eighteenth century renowned for his erudition and wisdom. Does a person's education provide him the qualities of mind that Cardinal Newman in *The Idea of a University* identifies as the attributes of intellectual excellence: "A habit of mind is formed which lasts through life, of which the attributes are, freedom, equitableness, calmness, moderation, and wisdom." If strength, stamina, energy, and agility mark a wholesome body, a healthy, flourishing mind also possesses telltale signs that reflect its vitality and vigor.

Just as the body can be malnourished or underfed, the mind also can be deficient. The mind can be in a state of vacancy or emptiness, craving food for thought and invigorating stimulation. Just as the body requires a well-balanced diet to perform its natural functions, the mind too requires nourishment from many sources to fulfill its proper activity of thinking. "Nothing can come from nothing," as Lucretius said. The mind needs raw material in order to build thoughts. A vacant or empty mind lacking necessary food and invigorating stimulation becomes a prey to what Dr. Johnson in *Rasselas* calls "the dangerous prevalence of the imagination," that is, the tendency to escape from reality by fantasizing, by creating a make-believe or alternative reality to replace the world as it is—the human condition, "the nature of things". Because nature abhors a vacuum, the void of the empty mind soon becomes filled with imaginary, fanciful illusions that distort the nature of reality and twist the truth of things. This daydreaming, then, invents utopias, creates unrealistic hopes, develops irrational fears, magnifies the importance of one person's work in the world, ignores the fallen nature of the world, or exaggerates the power of evil.

In Johnson's short novel *Rasselas* a young prince confined to the small world of The Happy Valley where he has lived a secluded life suffers from the problem of the empty or vacant mind. He complains of being "burdened with myself" as he finds himself in a state of mind lacking the necessary food for thought. Rasselas experiences boredom, idleness, melancholy, and fantasies as he inhabits both a limited physical world surrounded by mountains and dwells in a small mental world reduced to the same old images day after day and year after year. All the old pleasures have lost their novelty and ceased to please. Rasselas complains, "By possessing all that I can want, I find one day and one hour exactly like another, except that the latter is still more tedious than the former." In short, Rasselas' mind cannot grow because he lacks the necessary stimulation and fresh energy which new images provide. A mind filled with the same images, pictures, lessons, and experiences from a repetitious routine creates a stagnant condition. Rasselas hungers and craves for knowledge supplied only by leaving The Happy Valley and acquiring the variety of learning and experience that forms the healthy, invigorated state of mind Johnson calls "a mind replete with images".

Once Rasselas chooses to leave the Happy Valley, his entire state of mind grows and improves because his intelligence is active and searching. He seeks a way to escape the narrowness of The Happy Valley and then to explore the wide world to discover "the choice of life"—the secret to human happiness. A healthy mind is occupied and engaged in accomplishing some goal and anticipating some achievement in the future. As Rasselas says, ". . . I fancy I should be happy if I had something to pursue" and "give me something to desire." In the course of his travels Rassleas provides his mind with the raw material of thought. He stocks his mind with new images that come from the three traditional sources of knowledge: experience, learning, and reason. He mingles with people from all social classes from great political leaders like the Bassa of Egypt to humble figures like shepherds and a hermit. He associates with people of all ages from the young men of Cairo to old astronomers, and he mixes with individuals with differing degrees of learning from ignorant shepherds and simpleminded maids to learned Stoic philosophers and scientists experimenting with flying. He observes many pursuits of happiness from the pastoral life to the monastic life to the marital state, and he learns of the many theories of happiness from the Epicurean to the Stoic to the doctrine of "return to nature". Thus Rasselas's empty or stagnant mind is animated because of the newness of the stimuli and variety of the images. He comments to his sister, "Variety is so necessary to content that even the happy valley disgusted me by the recurrence of its luxuries." This variety of plentiful images provides a rich soil and ample nourishment for the mind to grow. As A.D. Sertillanges explains in *The Intellectual Life*: "Ideas emerge from facts; they also emerge from conversations, chance occurrences, theatres, visits, strolls, the most ordinary books. Everything holds treasures, because everything is in everything, and a few laws of life and of nature govern all the rest." The mind thrives on multiple images and needs a form of balanced nourishment similar to the diet that the healthy body requires.

Now that the mind is "replete with images" from travel, conversation, experience, and learning (and from strolls, conversations, and visits), the intellect performs its function of combining and distinguishing the images as it compares, contrasts, discerns, and judges all of the data it has assimilated. The intellect discovers its power as it acts upon the images, seeing similarities and distinctions, comparing the past with the present, and drawing generalizations and conclusions based upon real facts and human experiences—not from abstract theories or untested ideas. Imlac, the wise sage who becomes Rasselas's mentor, explains to him the relationship between knowledge and happiness: "I am less unhappy than the rest because I have a mind replete with images which I can vary and combine at pleasure. I can amuse my solitude by the renovation of the knowledge which begins to fade form memory, and by recollection of the accidents of my past life." In other words, with a plentiful variety of images, the mind can remember, reflect, reconsider, and contemplate—acquiring new insight, rediscovering old truths in a fresh ways, receiving more confirmation, and gaining greater convictions about the unchanging truths of human nature. With a mind constantly filled with new images added to old ideas and earlier memories, the mind acquires an interior life that values silence—another sign of a healthy intellect. As Imlac acknowledges, "But pleasures never can be so multiplied or continued, as not to leave much of life unemployed." A healthy mind possesses the resources of occupying itself and not needing constant diversion and entertainment. As A.D. Sertillanges writes in *The Intellectual Life*: "Prophets, apostles, preachers, martyrs, pioneers of knowledge, inspired artists in every art, ordinary men and the Man-God all pay tribute to loneliness, to the life of silence, to the night." A healthy mind in an atmosphere of quietness enjoys the activity of thinking, recollection, and contemplation and acquires a repose or tranquility that combats the restlessness and boredom that afflicted Rasselas in The Happy Valley. A healthy mind, A.D. Sertillanges notes, can easily retire to itself as it recognizes "the right balance between the life within and the life without, between silence and sound."

However, the primary purpose for the mind's need to be filled and replenished with images is not the cure of idleness, boredom, or restlessness but the discovery of the truth. The serenity and equanimity that a mind replete with images gains follow from the possession of the truth. As Johnson writes in *Preface to Shakespeare*, "The mind can only rest on the stability of truth." After Rasselas stocks his mind with the variety of images he acquires from his travels and conversations, he begins to compare and contrast them. First, he learns that no one is perfectly happy. The hermit complains that he finds solitude irksome and tedious "because I have no opportunities of relaxation and diversion." The shepherds living the pastoral life are "cankered with discontent" because they harbor envy for the rich. The rich experience no greater degree of happiness than the hermit or the shepherd because the wealthy prince confesses, "My condition has the appearance of happiness, but appearances are delusive. My prosperity puts my life in danger." Even the virtuous and the good are not guaranteed greater worldly happiness than the wicked. As Rasselas's sister Nekayah explains, war, famine, and tempest affect everyone the same: "But this, at least, may be maintained, that we do not always find visible happiness in proportion to visible virtue." From interpreting these images Rasselas discovers universal truths—another sign of a healthy mind which grasps first principles, eternal laws, and the unchanging nature of things. The mind of great poets possesses this quality as Imlac explains: they "must consider right and wrong in their abstract and invariable state" and must "disregard present laws and opinions and rise to general and transcendental truths, which will always be the same." No human being enjoys perfect happiness in his mortal life. This universal truth that Rasselas discovers from his many images cures him of his fantasies and utopian wishes, "the dangerous prevalence of the imagination" he revealed in The Happy Valley when he dreamed that his heroic adventures would culminate in victory and goodness as "his benevolence always terminated his projects in the relief of distress, the detection of fraud, the defeat of oppression, and the diffusion of happiness." In other words, Rasselas's healthy mind informed with real images from experience and observation corrects his abstract, untested theory about finding the ideal "choice of life". All these various examples provide living proof that contradicts the illusions about human happiness that daydreaming philosophers and poets invent.

Rasselas's travels and thoughts lead to another universal truth discovered from the food for thought his broad liberal education in the wide world provides. He learns that although utopia does not exist in the human world and stops seeking the perfect "choice of life," there are greater or lesser degrees of happiness. From the multitude of his images he not only compares and sees similarities but also distinguishes and sees significant differences. This ability to discern both resemblances and distinctions marks intellectual excellence with the attribute of good judgment, the fine art of discrimination. Although Rasselas admits that human life is a condition in which "much is to be endured and little to be enjoyed" for all people in all places, he reasons that human choices determine the various comparative degrees of happiness. In his debate with Nekayah about the happiness of the marital state, Rasselas accuses his sister of exaggeration and imbalance in recording only the sorrows and problems of marriage. She reports that the blindness of love, the battle of the sexes, and the conflict of the generations produce marriages that are merely tolerated and endured, not cherished as sources of true happiness. She concludes, "I know not . . . whether marriage be more than one of the innumerable modes of human misery." Rasselas criticizes his sister's simplistic, distorted view which lacks the art of exact distinction: "Both conditions may be bad, but they cannot both be the worst."

From his travels Rasselas has discovered the truth about human happiness that Imlac summarized in narrating the story of his life: ". . . we grow more happy as our minds take a wider range." In leaving The Happy Valley and entering the broad realm of travel, Rasselas enlarged his world. His happiness increased as his world widened. In conversing with the hermit, Rasselas recalls how the narrow world of solitude contributed to the man's misery: "In solitude, if I escape the example of bad men, I want likewise the counsel and conversation of the good." The hermit vows to leave his isolation and enter the larger world of human society to increase his happiness: "I have long been comparing the evils with the advantages of society, and resolve to return into the world tomorrow." Thus, learning from the images that equate happiness to the broadening of one's experience and the enlarging of one's social relationships, Rasselas reasons with clarity and conviction, "Marriage is evidently the dictate of nature; men and women were made to be the companions of one another, and therefore I cannot be persuaded but that marriage is one of the means of happiness." From his travels Rasselas understands the first principles of happiness and knows the universal truths that explain the causes of misery. A healthy intellect, then, organizes the myriad images of the mind to see recurring patterns that lead to conclusions and general truths about the permanent nature of things. Thus a social life, a busy purposeful life, a love of knowledge, and a varied life lead to more happiness than the seclusion of a hermit, an idle life of comfort in The Happy Valley, an ignorant mind that does not grow, and a monotonous life that lacks new images. The truth that no form of human happiness offers perfection leads to the higher truth that "the choice of eternity" is man's true hope for the fulfillment of man's infinite desires for pure happiness.

Along with overcoming the void of an empty, stagnant mind in need of new, varied images so it does not "grow muddy for want of motion," the intellect must safeguard itself from overspecialization, from acquiring a mind filled with images from the same field of learning or from only one source of knowledge. To be confined to science or philosophy without the benefit of travel, experience, and conversation leads to "airy notions" divorced from reality. In *Rasselas* a scientist who experiments with flying by devising wings, jumping from a mountain, and flapping the wings to keep afloat finds himself terrified and shocked when he falls with a crash: "he waved his pinions a while to gather air, then leaped from his stand, and in an instant dropped into the lake." This scientist needed the corrective of human experience to counteract his abstract theory of flying. His mind was not vacant but overfilled with images from one specialized branch of learning that distorted his perception of reality. Another scientist, the astronomer, also suffers from the problem of overspecialization as he limits his images to the ideas gleaned from one body of knowledge. His obsession with weather and astronomy has developed into an illusion that he controls the weather and governs the seasons. When the mind is not properly balanced with the right proportion of varied images from different branches of learning, the dangers of the imagination prevail, a condition where "all power of fancy over reason is a degree of insanity." The astronomer loses touch with reality because he exaggerates his importance and imagines himself having godlike authority in ruling the planets and the heavens. Because his mind lacks the checks and balances which a variety of images provides, he lacks a realistic perspective of his role in the world. Imlac reminds him of the hard truth: . . . "you are only one atom in the mass of humanity, and have neither such virtue nor vice as that you should be singled out for supernatural favours or afflictions." The astronomer dwells in the realm of speculation—his ideas having no correspondence with truth—because he has derived all his images from books and formal learning and deprived himself of the quintessential human experiences. He confesses, "I have passed my time in study without experience. . . . I have purchased knowledge at the expenses of all the common comforts of life: I have missed the endearing elegance of female friendship and the happy commerce of domestic tenderness." Theory without practice, books without experience, and work without play all rob the mind of its vigor and vitality. As A. D. Sertillanges explains, "a dry fruit" refers to "one whose mind is shrunken and shriveled because he has prematurely confined himself to the cultivation of one department of study."

The life of the mind, then, thrives when the healthy food of the mind nourishes it; when it inhabits a larger universe instead of a narrow world; when fresh new images are replenishing the old stale ones; when it is filled with images from a variety of sources that include books and travel, a knowledge of men and manners, and conversation and familiarity with all social classes; and when the mind keeps in motion and avoids complacency and stagnation. After being properly nourished and supplied, a healthy mind compares and contrasts, discerns and distinguishes, and seeks and discovers universal truths. Just as Michelangelo saw a David in a hunk of rock and seized the form from the matter, the healthy mind discovers form and shape—unity in multiplicity—as it reduces the many images to first principles and "general and transcendental truths which will always be the same".

However, in addition to the wholesome food gleaned from a variety of the best images and the vigorous exercise of comparing and contrasting those images, the intelligence also requires healthy air. As G. K. Chesterton remarked, fifty percent of education is atmosphere. Because learning is a serious, dignified, and noble activity, it requires an environment that is more formal than casual. Learning thrives in an atmosphere that reflects order, discipline, and propriety, in a place that evokes the tranquility of beauty, the recollection of silence, and the graciousness of civility and good taste. Without this aura of respect and reverence for learning, education descends to the level of the ultra casual and the informal—no different than watching a sports event on television—and loses its power to elevate the mind. The atmosphere of learning needs to resist the endless distractions of modern life and popular culture, whether it is cell phones in the classroom, garish clothing, immodest dress, or the noise of late arrivals or eating and drinking in class. Of the four basic skills represented by the traditional curriculum of the liberal arts, the *quadrivium*—reading, writing, speaking, and listening—the discipline of listening has suffered dramatically in this academic culture of informality because the atmosphere of video culture with its graphic pictures and sound bytes diverts the mind from reflection and contemplation. The atmosphere of learning also needs to restore the idea of play and leisure, that is, the enjoyment of learning as an end in itself that is inherently enjoyable and desirable for its own sake rather than as a means to an end—a marketable skill having a utilitarian value in the marketplace. As Blessed Cardinal Newman explains in *The Idea of a University*, anything that a person loves and relishes for the pure, sheer delight of the activity always abounds in fruitfulness:

> Good is not only good, but reproductive of good; this is one of its attributes; nothing is excellent, beautiful, perfect, desirable for its

> own sake, but it overflows, and spreads the
> likeness of itself all around. Good is prolific;
> it is not only good to the eye, but to the taste;
> it not only attracts us, but it communicates
> itself. . . . A great good will impart great good.

Consider the atmosphere of a typical scene from a
high school or college classroom in contemporary life.
Casual attire, baseball caps worn backward, students
arriving late or coming and going to restrooms in endless
procession all interrupt the attention and concentration
of thinking. The mind cannot soar, focus, or even
listen in such an environment. This is what Chesterton
means when he says that fifty percent of education is
atmosphere. If the environment reflects decorum,
dignity, seriousness, and formality, learning comes more
easily and naturally. When learning resembles watching
a movie in the relaxation of the family room or viewing
the Super Bowl in the company of drinking companions,
it loses its special aura and becomes trivial.

What are the images that fill the mind of students these
days? Are students introduced to the great, memorable
images that illuminate the meaning of the true, good,
and beautiful, or are their minds empty of such pictures
of nobility, chivalry, purity, and civility? As Thomas
Howard, a great Catholic writer of our time writes, the
images that fill the minds of the young present "MTV,
rock music, lewd cinema, pornography" and consist of
messages from "the omnipotent conspiracy of the whole
of academia, political power, and the media" which
promote "a sensuality that makes Gomorrah itself look
like Mr. McGregor's garden." Are the images of popular
culture that enter the minds of students "the best that

has been thought and said" in Matthew Arnold's famous phrase or the worst and lowest of what has been thought and said? Do students have deposited in their minds good books, beautiful music, glorious art and architecture, civilized conversation, and examples of courtesy, modesty, nobility, and sanctity? Are the images primarily from one source—video games, television programs, Hollywood films, Internet, and advertising—or are the ideas that fill the mind derived from the perennial sources of traditional knowledge that produce the sound mind in the sound body filled with ideas both from work and play, formal learning and informal experience, from the permanence of home and the enrichment of travel, and from the knowledge received through the senses and the learning acquired by the mind? It is imperative to remember that "nothing can come from nothing" and that "nature abhors a vacuum". If the mind is not properly nourished and lacks the substantial food for thought, it cannot think or discover the truth. Without the knowledge of the truth, the fantasies of the imagination begin to fill the impoverished mind which only remains empty until some popular slogan or propaganda or "virtual reality" or sophisticated lie substitutes itself for the truth. In Orwell's *1984* this technique of manipulation is known as Thought Control. Throughout the novel all the beautiful images of the past, all the sublime moral ideals of Christianity, all the great books of Western civilization have to be banned and censored to purge the mind of this wholesome content so that the empty mind can be fed with the lies, nonsense, and the propaganda of ideology. As the main character Winston says of one brainwashed character, "She had not a thought in her head that was not a slogan, and there was no imbecility, absolutely

14

none, that she was not capable of swallowing if the Party handed it out to her." If the mind is not nourished with the real food of the mind in the home, in the school, and in the church, it will subsist on the junk food of political correctness that repeats in slogans and clichés the cant of diversity, multiculturalism, reproductive freedom, and sexual liberation. Without a mind replete with images of goodness, beauty, and truth from nature, home, tradition, religion, and great literature, art, and music, the mind will lack the resources to discover the splendor of the truth which gives equanimity to the mind, joy to the spirit, and the happiness of contemplation to the mind.

Chapter 2. The Fullness of the Truth and the Sin of Sloth

G. K. Chesterton once compared the richness and completeness of the Catholic faith to an estate. Distinguishing between the virtue of appreciating "something in everything" and the art of discovering "everything in something," Chesterton found in the Catholic faith the fullness of the truth that he compared to the copiousness of a great estate. What if one found all the parts in the integrity of the whole instead of recovering the many fragments and splinters in various places? What if the quiet of the Quaker, the enthusiasm of the Methodist, the opulence of Eastern orthodoxy, the traditionalism of the Anglican, and the Protestant love of God's Word were all synthesized in one church? This economy would make a church "the pearl of great price," a beautiful work of art in which all the different parts form a unified, harmonious whole and a repository of the whole truth in all of its splendor instead of a fragmentation of broken pieces without design or unity. Referring to a convert like himself, Chesterton explains, "[E}xperience has taught him that he will find nearly everything somewhere inside that estate and that a very large number of people are finding nothing outside it. For the estate is not only a formal garden or an ordered farm; there is plenty of hunting and fishing on it, and, as the phrase goes, very good sport."

Without the fullness of the truth and the unity of the faith, the error of indifferentism develops: one church or religion is as good as another. Truth becomes relative, culturally or politically determined, and as variable as the multitude of human opinions. As the liberal Dr. Brownside in Newman's *Loss and Gain* explains, "We can't do without some outward form of belief; one is not truer than another, that is, all are equally true. . . . All are true. . . . That is the better way of taking it; none are shams, all are true." Thus what Newman calls "liberalism" spreads the seeds of heresy and dissent which divide the unity of Christendom, fragment the universality of truth, and undermine moral authority. Rejecting the Magisterium of the Catholic Church and the infallibility of the popes on the matters of faith and morals, the Christian world spawns moral dissension and teaches contradictory truths which inevitably sow discord and provoke cultural wars. The only expedient, then, to this moral and intellectual anarchy is the appeal to tolerance, an attempt to circumvent thought by denying that heretical ideas have dangerous and destructive consequences.

Without the fullness of the truth that resides in the Petrine office, one might be anti-abortion but pro-contraception. One might recognize the sacramental, indissoluble nature of Christian marriage but neglect the obligation to be generous with life. One might honor the religious heritage and traditions of one's parents and ancestors but never fully grasp the universality of the Christian religion or recognize the meaning behind the words "one, holy, catholic, and apostolic." One might love God's Word in Sacred Scripture but fail to grasp the awesome mystery of the Holy Sacrifice of the Mass. One might honor the Ten Commandments and the Sermon on the Mount but never encounter the great spiritual classics like Augustine's *Confessions*, Thomas a Kempis's *The Imitation of Christ*, and St. Francis de Sales' *Introduction to a Devout Life*. One might believe in God as an "unmoved mover" or "first principle" or perfect clockmaker but never discover the breadth and depth of divine love or the infinite mercy of the Sacred Heart which loves each person "as if he were the only one," to paraphrase St. Augustine.

Instead of struggling to find the truth in the tortured anguish of an Augustine in the *Confessions* or undergoing the emotional turmoil of a Newman in *Apologia Pro Vita Sua* or wandering through the labyrinthine ways of a Francis Thompson in "The Hound of Heaven," a person can receive the fullness or unity of the truth in a more natural and perfect way. Like the Word made Flesh, the Magisterium of the Catholic Church is "the true light, which enlighteneth every man that cometh into the world" (John 1: 9). There are two ways of gaining knowledge: the transmission of truth and wisdom by way of moral authority, divine revelation, and authentic tradition or the discovery of knowledge by way of failure, tragedy, and suffering. The first is the way of innocence and the second the way of experience. Because of the perversity of fallen human nature, man all too often chooses the hard way of experience, repeating the mistakes of the past or of others instead of humbly receiving the wisdom of the ages or the infallible authority of the Magisterium. In the Fall, Adam and Eve gained their knowledge of good and evil by way of experience—the eating of the forbidden fruit—instead of by way of obedience to God's commandment.

The moral crisis of the late twentieth and twenty-first centuries illustrates the knowledge of experience gained from a fall. In the *Poetics* Aristotle calls the essence of tragedy "recognition" (*anagnorosis*)—the shocking discovery of a self-evident moral truth through suffering, a knowledge that never required the trauma of evil or the bitterness of experience to gain the wisdom. In every case the fullness of the truth found in the Catholic Church forewarned of the grave evils and tragic outcomes precipitated by indifferentism, the notion that one religion is as authoritative as another and that all moral traditions and "choices" are equal. The decadence that has followed the sexual revolution of the past fifty years from contraception to abortion to divorce to homosexuality violates the perennial teaching of the Church on the immorality of contraception. Obedience to *Humanae Vitae* would have resisted the moral decline in sexual morality that has created the culture of death—sexuality divorced from life, love, and commitment and a contraceptive, anti-life mentality that requires abortion as an alternative form of birth control.

All the prophetic statements of that encyclical are incontrovertible: ". . . a road would thus be opened to conjugal infidelity and a general lowering of morality." In *The Index of Leading Cultural Indicators*, William J. Bennett writes, "Since 1960, illegitimate births have increased more than 400 percent." Paul VI also warned, "It can also be feared that the man who becomes used to contraceptive practices may finally lose respect for the woman. . . considering her as a mere instrument of selfish enjoyment, and no longer his respected and beloved companion." The contraceptive mentality has caused the fatherless families where men use and abandon women. In *The Index* William Bennett's sources from the U. S. Bureau of the Census document this trend: "The percent of children living in single-parent homes has more than tripled in the last three decades." The Pope also prophesied of "the dangerous weapon that would thus be placed in the hands of those public authorities who have no concern for the requirements of morality." The draconian population control policy of China and the aggressive population control measures of the United Nations and other agencies in promoting abortion, sterilization, and contraception in third world nations by way of "foreign aid" or "development" again verify the fullness of the truth found in Catholic teaching.

Sociologists document the harmful effects of divorce to men, women, children, and society in books like Barbara Whitehead's *The Culture of Divorce* and Maggie Gallagher's *The Abolition of Marriage*. Again the venerable, time-tested truths of the Christian tradition are re-learned from bitter experience instead of acquired from innocence and obedience. While different denominations offer conflicting views on the morality of divorce and civil law promotes no-fault, easy divorce and the laws of the land acknowledge cohabiting "domestic partners" as the equivalent of a married man and woman, the Catholic Church has always taught the indissolubility of marriage. The consequences of the sexual revolution again prove the infallible wisdom of the Church. Honoring the perennial teaching of the Church on the sanctity and sacramental nature of marriage would have prevented the crisis of the family that has tortured the lives of the young and disintegrated the home, the center of civilization. Fatherless America and the single-parent family have created a host of pathologies for the young that Urie Bronfenbrenner of Cornell University summarizes:

. . . a variety of behavioral and educational problems, including extremes of hyperactivity and withdrawal; lack of attentiveness in the classroom; difficulty in deferring gratification; impaired academic achievement; school misbehavior, absenteeism; dropping out; involvement in socially alienated peer groups, and the so-called 'teenage-syndrome' of behaviors that tend to hang together— smoking, drinking, early and frequent sexual experience, and in the more extreme cases, drugs, suicide, vandalism, violence, and criminal acts.

Again it is the fullness of Catholic moral teaching in its foresight and infallibility that protects man from the self-destruction and tragedy that follow from indifferentism or "pluralism" in the modern politically correct sense.

While social planners, eugenicists, and alarmists are obsessed with population control, small families, and sterilization, the Church proclaims the fruitfulness of love and the virtue of generosity with life. As the Western world believed the doomsday prophecies of Paul Ehrlich's *The Population Bomb* and ignored God's command to "be fruitful and multiply" and rejected the Catholic Church's teaching about the openness to new human life, it suffered the consequences of a birth dearth, not the multiplication of billions which the earth could not feed. As Western European nations fail to replace themselves with low average birth rates of 1.3 to 1.7 children per family instead of the minimum 2.1 necessary for populations to remain stable, they deprive themselves of their greatest resources—the people who will become producers, consumers, taxpayers, soldiers, and laborers, not to mention their special talents, gifts, and genius. While the Church teaches that a Divine Providence numbers the hairs on the head of every person and cares for the fall of a sparrow and warns man not to be anxious about tomorrow, social engineers panic about the shortage of food and energy and envision a world of teeming billions that will pollute the quality of life and destroy the environment. Thus when man accepts the notion of acknowledging "something in everything" by seeking the truth in piecemeal style instead of embracing the ideal of "everything in something" by turning to the God who is one, to the church which is universal, or to the authority which is infallible, then man lives a divided life without integrity, suffering what T.S. Eliot called "dissociation of sensibility."

This intellectual schizophrenia deconstructs the harmony of nature and the integrity of human nature. For example, contraception separates love and life, severing the bond between the unitive and procreative aspects of love. Divorce tears asunder what God has joined together. Population control separates the head and the heart, the mind's utilitarian logic accepting theories and abstractions instead of obeying the dictates of the heart to give and love generously. Abortion and euthanasia also compromise morality and integrity by undermining the unity of the moral act, the simple teaching that one may never do evil to accomplish good. Feminist ideology destroys the complementarity of maleness and femaleness by denigrating fatherhood and identifying patriarchy as the root of all evil: children do not need the influence of both a father and a mother to live a balanced life shaped by love and discipline, justice and mercy, strength and gentleness instilled by the love of two parents. The fullness of the truth, then, achieves this equilibrium of unifying and coordinating disparate parts to eliminate extremes and one-sidedness which inevitably follow from indifferentism. Without the fullness of the truth, ideologies develop which distort or exaggerate a portion of the truth at the expense of the whole.

Whereas the Catholic Church honors the dignity of the person and defends the sacredness of life, rejecting the mentality that views man as a means to an end and which measures his worth in terms of utilitarian categories such as productiveness, cost effectiveness, and quality of life, the modern world cheapens and debases human life. In the culture of death humans are destroyed by contraceptive abortifacients, surgical abortions, and physician-assisted suicide. Biotechnology experiments with aborted babies and engages in medical research through fetal harvesting as human life becomes reduced to fetal "matter" and "tissue." The dignity of the human being consists in the fact that he is a union of body and soul, a mortal creature with a divine destiny, an image of God who cannot be used, manipulated, or treated as a means to an end. Without this truth of the Catholic faith, man becomes an object subject to utilitarian motives or an animal liable to experimentation. As St. Pope John Paul II writes in *Evangelium Vitae*, ". . . the use of embryos or fetuses as an object of experimentation constitutes a crime against their human dignity as human beings, who have a right to the same respect owed to a child once born, just as to every person." Without this truth defending "the absolute inviolability of innocent human life," killing in all its overt and subtle forms assumes a respectable normalcy because of legalization. The horrors of partial-birth abortion and physician-assisted suicide and the link between abortion and breast cancer and the relationship between contraception and cancer all result from the rejection of the Church's teaching in its fullness: every human life from conception until death is sacred; abortion is always intrinsically evil; man is never a means to an end. In John Paul II's words, "I confirm that the direct and voluntary killing of an innocent human being is always gravely immoral" (*Evangelium Vitae*, #57).

These moral truths are universal and have been consistently taught and reaffirmed throughout the ages. The history of the late twentieth century proves that obedience to the Magisterium prevents the tragedies of making fatal mistakes and learning painful moral lessons through the bitter experience of suffering and loss. Every deviation from the fullness of the truth in its integrity exacts an enormous price in human misery. Just as the Bible is a book of love because God reveals Himself as the Word (the Truth) in all its light and glory, the Magisterium is another book of God's love which illuminates the splendor of truth. God does not abandon the children He loves. He provides unchanging moral principles, absolute truths, and universal norms in times of moral confusion and ideological culture wars. Like a loving father He teaches His children and transmits to them the wisdom of the ages that will make them free and happy. He does not leave them in darkness. The meaning of right and wrong are always clear. Why, then, does man not see the light? Blessed Cardinal Newman in his sermon, "Truth Hidden When Not Sought After," addresses this dilemma.

Selecting a text from II Timothy 4:4, "They shall turn away their ears from the truth, and shall be turned unto fables," Newman observes that "the multitude of men are wrong" on matters of religion truth because of the diversity of creeds, sects, and authorities. If religion is one, Newman argues, then "all views of religion but one are wrong." However, Newman also acknowledges that the "few" are often as wrong as the "many" in matters of religious knowledge:

> But on the contrary, let us honestly confess what is certain, that not the ignorant, or weakminded, or dull, or enthusiastic, or extravagant only turn their ears from the truth and are turned unto fables, but also men of powerful minds, keen perceptions, extended views, ample and various knowledge.

For Newman many stumbling blocks lead the learned and the scholarly to reject the fullness of the truth and to turn to fables. First, "Christian revelation addresses itself to our hearts, to our love of truth and goodness, our fear of sinning, and our desire to gain God's favor." Intellectual acumen and scholarly achievements reflect excellent mental powers, Newman admits, but they do not necessarily bestow religious wisdom any more than the possession of God's truth qualifies a person to know a foreign language or discover a scientific law. The educated or elite few who are endowed with "brilliant mental endowments," Newman reasons, resist God's truths for various reasons: "it is bad men, proud men, men of hard hearts, and unhumbled tempers, and immoral lives, these are they who reject the Gospel." In other words, as sin darkens the intellect and disorders the will, man loses his taste for the simple desire of truth for its own sake, the natural love of goodness for its beautiful attraction, and the purity of heart which leads to a knowledge of God. The theologians who dissent from *Human Vitae*, the medical professionals who promote the contraceptive mentality and the culture of death, and the courts that invent imaginary "rights" exemplify the "few" with powerful minds who illustrate how the experts can be as blind to the truth as the masses.

Newman cites another reason for men's preference for darkness over light—the sin of sloth: "If men turn unto fables of their own will, they do it on account of their pride, or their love of indolence and self-indulgence." The symptoms of the deadly sin of *acedia* are carelessness or indifference in matters of religious truth, negligence in seeking the truth with all of one's mind, heart, strength, and will, and lack of earnestness in a matter of supreme importance. Newman excoriates this lack of effort and will power:

> Doubtless if men sought the truth with one tenth part of the zeal with which they seek to acquire wealth or secular knowledge, their differences would diminish year by year. Doubtless if they gave a half or a quarter of the time to prayer for Divine guidance which they give to amusement or recreation, or which they give to dispute and contention, they would be ever approximating each other.

Thus the preoccupation with pleasure ("safe sex"), with ease (no-fault divorce), convenience (abortion on demand), with self-esteem ("I'm OK, you're OK), with consumerism (two-income families), and with multiculturalism (all truth is relative) promotes the insidiousness of sloth that refuses to exert the will or the mind to discern the truth or resolve the issues of good and evil. The passionate love of goodness or justice degenerates to the level of being "moderate" (read: neutral) or condoning "choice," and the outrage toward the ugliness of evil is reduced to a matter of tolerance. When men are neither hot nor cold, God will vomit them as the book of Revelation declares. Given the fullness of the truth, given the Light of the Gospel and the Word made Flesh, given the infallible Magisterium of the Church on matters of faith and morals, given the crisis in marriage and the family, and given the decadence and the violence of the culture of death in all its atrocities from AIDS to infanticide to physician-assisted suicide, how can men turn away their ears from God and turn to fables when the truth is crying aloud on the housetops?

The correspondence between the vice of sloth and the rejection of the fullness of the truth is a benchmark of modernity. On the one hand, Christian denominations teach conflicting truths about divorce, contraception, abortion, and homosexuality, and secular ideologies reject the fundamental truths of the Christian faith as mere religious opinions without authority. On the other hand, the sin of sloth prevails on all levels of the culture from the Supreme Court of the United States refusing to uphold the universal meaning of marriage as the union of one man and one woman to members of Congress "being personally opposed to abortion but . . ." to institutions of higher learning lowering academic and moral standards to parents expecting government programs and daycare to raise their children to low birth rates in which Western nations cannot even be awakened from their somnolence to replace themselves. Dante in the *Inferno* depicts the punishment of the slothful as the torment of bees and wasps goading them into activity as the lazy are driven to rally around a flag or cause with zeal and fortitude. In the *Purgatorio* Dante portrays the slothful as in a state of running to overcome the inertia that paralyzed their good works in their mortal life. The connection is clear: passion in the form of love for the truth and for God—the "zeal" and "earnestness" Newman recommends—is also the antidote to the disorder of sloth. No one can discover the fullness of the truth or recognize the great estate in which one finds "everything in something" without the intensity of a Julius Caesar whose legions astonished their enemies by their incredible speed or without the alacrity of the Blessed Virgin Mary who heard the news of Elizabeth's conception and instantly rushed to do good—two examples cited by Dante as the remedies to sloth. As Newman (quoting from Proverbs 2: 3-5) testifies, "If thou criest after knowledge, and liftest up thy voice for understanding; if thou seekest her as silver, and searchest for her as for hid treasures; then shalt thou understand the fear of the Lord, and find the knowledge of God." Comprehending the fullness of the truth and conquering sloth demand nothing less than the fire of love that seeks Him "with the whole heart" as Newman concludes in his sermon.

Chapter 3. The Perennial Philosophy versus Ideology

If a culture rejects the wisdom of the past—the natural law, the perennial philosophy, the Ten Commandments, the classical-Christian tradition, and the classics ("the best that has been thought and said," as Matthew Arnold said)—an enormous void appears. Because nature abhors a vacuum, the ancient truths and eternal verities do not disappear and leave nothing behind. As Blessed Cardinal Newman explained in *The Idea of a University*, if theology is no longer studied as a body of knowledge in the curriculum of a liberal arts course, then other bodies of knowledge compete for the territory formerly ruled by the queen of the sciences:

> If you drop any science of the circle of knowledge, you cannot keep its place vacant for it; that science is forgotten; the other sciences close up, or, in other words, they exceed their proper bounds, and intrude where they have no right . . .; and if Theology is not allowed to occupy its own territory, adjacent sciences, nay, sciences which are quite foreign to Theology, will take possession of it.

G. K. Chesterton also stated the same idea: no man can believe in "nothing". If he does not believe in the universal truths and moral norms common to all cultures, then he will believe in "anything," that is, heresy, superstition, or propaganda. Error will fill the void left by truth. The traditional moral teachings and timeless truths of Western civilization have been subverted by a myriad of ideologies that have created the phenomenon of political correctness. These ancient truths have been stigmatized as mere religious opinion, as dead white men's philosophy, as Eurocentrism, as sexism, racism, and homophobia. In the name of change, progress, revolution, and enlightenment, the old ("the permanent things") have been undermined by the avant-garde, the fashionable, and the radical. In short, the enduring universal truths of the perennial philosophy have been displaced by ideology, the new doctrines that have filled the void created by the deconstruction of the wisdom of the past.

How is it possible to assert, for example, that war, slavery, and ignorance are good rather than evil? "War is peace," "freedom is slavery," and "ignorance is strength"—the slogans in Orwell's *1984*—amount to contradictions like "up is down," "left is right," "male is female," "evil is good," and "false is true." In order for ideology to accomplish its revolution in morals and to occupy the vacuum left by the destruction of timeless truths, the organs of mass communication must be harnessed to disseminate propaganda by means of the media in all its forms. Universities, schools, textbooks, the press, the film industry, and television programming all popularize the slogans and catch phrases that pose as "truth". Feminist ideology (which equates women with men), the homosexual agenda (which equates same-sex marriage with heterosexual marriage), and liberal ideology (which equates minority cultures with

Western civilization) all rely upon verbal engineering to complement the social and moral revolution which their radical theories require. How can war be peace? How can two men or two women be "married"? By means of an intellectual revolution that, in effect, utters, in Satan's famous phrase from *Paradise Lost*, "Evil, be thou my good," ideology by a sleight of hand soon becomes commonplace and mainstream. The euphemisms of "Reproductive rights," "alternative lifestyles," and "no fault divorce" glamorize evil, and the pejorative terms "extremist," "homophobia" and "Eurocentrism" demonize traditional morality. Like the charlatans in Hans Andersen's "The Emperor's New Clothes" who are busy weaving, ideologues must produce a spate of words, articles, interviews, editorials, and books that repeat that the naked king is handsome. "It is beautiful. It is very lovely," mumbled the old prime minister in Andersen's story.

These moral revolutions, however, do not progress by means of slow development, organic growth, or due process. They are violent, cataclysmic dislocations that resemble the chaos and destruction of war—a cultural war. In normal change or natural development a line of continuity links the present with the past. The oak tree resembles the sapling; the fifty-year old man resembles the ten-year old boy he once was; the culture of the present day traces itself to its founding. However, in cultural revolutions all links between the present and the past are severed as the heritage and legacy of earlier ages are repudiated because they are "out of date," mythical, or biased. By one stroke, by one judicial decision of a supreme court legalizing abortion or same-sex unions, the law of the land and the culture of a civilization are changed overnight. In the coup of *Roe v. Wade* in 1973 in Washington, D.C., suddenly killing one's offspring is legal. In a similar coup in 2004 in Massachusetts and in the Supreme Court decision of *Obergefell v. Hodges* in 2015, marriage no longer means a union between a man and a woman.

Circumventing legislatures, moral consensus, and due process, ideology usurps the domain once occupied by truth and then imposes the Thought Police to censor any deviations from the slogans that propagate the new doctrines. Political correctness is enforced in the press, on television and radio stations, in the universities, in textbooks, and in films as these liberal bastions of ideology communicate the propaganda that subverts the moral wisdom of the ages. The invention of speech codes that forbid any legitimate criticism of the new morality and the establishment of hate crimes that punish the "intolerant" for discrimination enforce the dogmas of ideology. When Lawrence Summers, the president of Harvard University, proposed the idea of "innate differences" as an explanation for the small number of women employed in engineering and the sciences, he committed the unpardonable sin and suffered excoriation in the academic world. To condemn sodomy on the basis of religious authority and natural law or to uphold the sanctity of all human life as a self-evident truth common to civilized societies and the world's great religions likewise amounts to unconscionable bigotry in the politically correct universe. Hence, once the classical-Christian tradition loses its status as knowledge or wisdom worthy of perpetuation by means of tradition and education, other unqualified bodies of knowledge lay claim to expertise about good and evil.

All ideologies conform to the myth about the bed of Procrustes, the king who either stretched the legs of his short victims until they fit his bed or cut off the legs of his taller captives to make them the perfect size. Harsh and inflexible in fitting reality to his preconceived ideas, Procrustes never adjusted the bed in accordance with the nature of human beings. Likewise, ideologies torture and twist the real nature of things to force them to conform to some *idée fixe*. For example, men and women possess different but complementary natures. A woman can conceive and bear a child, but a man does not possess this capacity. This unfortunate state of affairs, according to feminist ideology and Supreme Court Justice Ruth Bader Ginsburg, requires legalized abortion so that women alone do not suffer the burden of childbearing which unjustly penalizes women and does not oppress men. The structure of reality, the maleness and femaleness of humans, must be attacked to accommodate an abstract theory that repudiates self-evident truths.

A marriage consists of a union of a man and a woman, but, according to the advocates of same-sex marriage, this arrangement is arbitrary and merely conventional, one in need of rearrangement to provide "equality under the law"—the rationale for Margaret Marshall's ruling in the Massachusetts Supreme Judicial Court and the U.S. Supreme Court's *Obergefell v. Hodges* decision. The nature and purpose of marriage, an institution founded for the procreation of children and the continuation of the human race, must be redefined and reorganized to wrench the obvious meaning of marriage as the bond of a man and woman for the sake of fatherhood and motherhood. The unnatural and immoral must be stretched and twisted to appear legitimate and respectable, and the time-honored and sacramental nature of holy matrimony must be desecrated to eliminate "discrimination".

The normative, universal meaning of a family, the most natural of all relationships, is defined as a father, mother, and children. But, according to the leftist ideology of the United Nations, families come in a myriad of forms: children and two mothers, children and two fathers, unwed mothers with children from different fathers. Mother Nature's simple plan for the well-being and best interests of children and society is contorted and mangled as new meanings of the family are wrested to accommodate special interests. Ideology, then, presuming to remake the world in its own image, never surrenders to the time-tested, God-given structure of reality or acknowledges the real nature of things.

Ideology never originates as a grassroots movement that reflects the common sense of ordinary people, *vox populi, vox dei* (the voice of the people, the voice of God)—what Edmund Burke calls "the moral sentiments," that is, "the common feelings of nature, as well as all sentiments of morality and religion." On the contrary, ideology begins with the elite and the educated classes and moves downward to the populace as it disseminates and popularizes its radical ideas and new morality. Just as in "The Emperor's New Clothes" the swindlers first persuaded the emperor at the top of the social hierarchy that they were weaving beautiful clothing for his kingship—a lie which "all the councilors, ministers, and men of great importance" also believe lest they appear ignorant or incompetent to judge—ideology proceeds from the upper classes to the common man—from Supreme Courts to ordinary people. As the king walked in procession before the crowds, they also agreed, "What a magnificent robe!" From the lie of the swindlers to the credulity of the king to the conformity of the court officials to the gullibility of the crowd, nonsense masquerades as sense because of each social class repeating, "It is magnificent! Beautiful! Excellent!" The proliferation of ideology also operates from the top down, from the intellectual and professional classes through the middle class to the average citizen. The style and clothes of trendy intellectual fashion soon set the tone, and political correctness becomes the rage. The great lies always begin with the talented and gifted intellectuals whose theoretical, abstract minds have lost contact with reality. In the words of G. K. Chesterton, while "the great poet only professes to express the thought that everybody has always had," philosophers like Kant, Hegel, Nietzsche and Marx "pretended to have a thought that nobody ever had." No one ever proposed or imagined the idea of human cloning, but scientists have seriously proposed the unthinkable. Edmund Burke in *Reflections on the Revolution in France* also warned against the propagators or "projectors" of radical ideas untested by time and experience: "We are afraid to put men to live and trade each on his own private stock of reason; because we suspect that this stock in each man is small, and that the individuals would do better to avail themselves of the general bank and capital of nations, and of ages." These novel ideas, however, soon circulate and gain respectability because of the influence of the philosophers and the *philosophes* and because of the power of the media, the courts, and the universities.

Modern universities and colleges, for example, are notorious for promoting radical ideologies such as Communism, feminism, homosexuality, and multiculturalism—all ideas which promote sameness and uniformity and ignore the qualitative distinctions that inhere in the structure of reality. Ideology, as the myth of Procrustes illustrates, thrives on the destruction of natural hierarchies and intrinsic differences that distinguish societies and individuals. Ideology seeks homogeneity or "leveling". In the name of *"liberte, egalite, fraternite"* the revolutionaries that instigated the French Revolution subjected to the guillotine entire social classes, the aristocracy and the priesthood. In the name of a classless society the radicals that precipitated the Communist Revolution also caused untold deaths and destroyed royalty and religion in Russia. In modern jargon this distortion of "leveling" has assumed the guise of "tolerance" and "equality under the law". However, as Dr. Johnson observed in Boswell's *Life of Johnson*, "Sir, your levelers wish to level *down* as far as themselves; but they cannot bear leveling *up* to themselves. They would all have some people under them; why not have some people above them?" Burke also recognized the absurdity of the leveling doctrine of the French Revolution that attempted to eliminate and reduce local customs and traditions to create a monolithic France that fit geometrical models: ". . . the geometrical policy has been adopted, that all local ideas should be sunk, and that the people should no longer be Gascons, Picards, Bretons, Normans, but Frenchmen with one country, one heart, and one assembly. But instead of all being Frenchmen, the greater likelihood is, that the inhabitants of that region will shortly have no country." In its prefabricated boxes, ideology blurs the normal, God-given differences that separate individuals, the sexes, societies, and cultures and mars the infinite variety, colorfulness, and richness of created things.

Ideology also carries on its cultural revolution by invoking "the rights of man," the cry of the French Revolution. Radical feminism justifies legalized abortion as "reproductive rights" or as "the right to privacy," and proponents of same-sex marriage rationalize their demands as a matter of civil rights due to all minorities. Advocates of euthanasia consider physician-assisted suicide as the right to die with dignity. In short, ideology invents rights that do not correspond to the nature and dignity of human beings and denies the simple truth that Burke succinctly formulates: "Men have no right to do what is not reasonable, and to what is not to their benefit." The rights of man demanded by ideology do not correspond to what Burke calls "the *real* rights of man" founded in human nature and civil society such as the right to life, property, liberty, and the pursuit of human happiness. Of course this fanaticism about imaginary absolute rights exaggerates the ideal of freedom to allow virtually anything in the name of "choice," whether it is abortion, euthanasia, or same-sex-marriage. The more that ideology glamorizes the revolutionary notion of "the rights of man" to justify self-aggrandizement, the more it denigrates moral duty as man's obligations to others.

None of the modern ideologies have any sense of the Roman ideal of *pietas* epitomized in Virgil's "pious Aeneas"—the hero of the *Aeneid* who left the burning city of Troy carrying his aged father on his shoulders and holding the hand of his young son to rescue them from tragedy. In C. S. Lewis's *The Abolition of Man* the natural law (what Lewis calls the Tao) acknowledges two major categories of duties that oblige all humans: "Duties to Parents, Elders, Ancestors" and "Duties to Children and Posterity". For example,

> Children, the old men, the poor, and the sick should be considered as the lords of the atmosphere. (Hindu. Janet, 1.8)
>
> I tended the old man, I gave him my staff (Ancient Egyptian. ERE v. 481)
>
> Great reverence is owed to a child. (Roman. Juvenal, xiv. 47)
>
> The master said, Respect the young. (Ancient Chinese. Analects. ix. 22)

In its pursuit of self-interest or power in the name of rights, freedom, or choice, ideology disavows the quintessential human obligations to respect and care for the young and the elderly. In short, the glorification of rights culminates in power, and the love of power produces tyranny and the mentality of "might makes right". The exercise of the imaginary rights espoused by ideologues denies the real rights of other persons. The imaginary right to slavery robs the black slave of his dignity. The imaginary "right to choice" in legalized abortion violates the pre-born child's right to life. The imaginary right to marriage and adoption claimed by homosexuals deprives children of a normal family shaped by the complementary virtues of both a father and a mother.

True wisdom, on the other hand, does not use Procrustes' bed as its paradigm. It acknowledges that human beings possess an innate, God-given, fixed, essential nature that directs their actions and purpose. In Dante's *Paradiso* Dante marvels at the quickness of his flight as he ascends through the heavenly spheres closer to the origin of all movement, God. Beatrice, his guide, explains that Dante's rapid spiritual progress toward God and truth is determined by his spiritual and moral nature to know and love God. It is no more unnatural than a stream of water moving downward because everything created has a nature, a nature that moves according to a wise design: "You should not, as I see it, marvel more/ at your ascent than at a river's fall/ from a high mountain to the valley floor." Man's spiritual, divine nature, then, forbids the exploitation, experimentation, and manipulation that cloning and fetal harvesting presume. Man by nature is born male or female, and this identity dictates a destiny of fatherhood or motherhood—a natural family that consists of a union of a man and a woman that rejects androgyny, homosexuality, and same-sex marriage. In short, true wisdom respects the created order as the wise plan of Mother Nature and as the providential design of God's intelligence. Whereas ideology operates under the premise that, in O'Brien's words from Orwell's *1984,* "Men are infinitely malleable," and that there is no such thing as a human nature in the universal sense, the classical-Christian tradition constantly affirms the reality of an unchangeable human nature. O'Brien, the Communist ideologue, insists, "We control life, Winston, at all levels. You are imagining that there is something called human nature which will be outraged by what we will do and will turn against us. But we create human nature." On the contrary, the classical

41

philosophy of Aristotle and St. Thomas Aquinas holds that man by nature desires to know, man by nature is a rational animal, man by nature is a political animal, and man by nature is godlike.

True wisdom honors the past and respects traditions, always building upon ancient foundations and preserving continuity. In Burke's words, "Besides, the people of England well know, that the idea of inheritance furnishes a sure principle of conservation, and a sure principle of transmission." Natural law and the perennial philosophy are not fashionable intellectual trends that come and go according to the times but enduring truths capable of development and refinement. The universal truths persist in all times, places, and cultures as C. S. Lewis illustrates in *The Abolition of Man.* All the moral precepts he cites—the law of beneficence, the law of magnanimity, the law of mercy, the law of good faith, the law of justice—derive from the sacred writings, philosophers, and religious traditions of all cultures from the Chinese to the Old Norse to the Hindu to the Babylonian to the Greeks and Romans to the Jews and Christians. This moral wisdom traces its continuity from the ancient world to modern times, from Sophocles to Cicero to St. Paul to St. Thomas Aquinas to the Catholic Church to C.S. Lewis. Antigone in Sophocles' play *Antigone* speaks of "the unwritten unalterable laws/ Of God and heaven. . . . They are not of yesterday or today, but everlasting." Cicero in *On Duties* writes, ". . . we are all subject to one and the same law of nature: and, that being so, the very least that such a law enjoins is that we must not wrong one another." St. Paul acknowledges that the Gentiles who do not know the divine law of the Ten Commandments nevertheless possess the knowledge of good and evil known to all men: "When Gentiles who have not the law do by nature what the law requires, they are a law to themselves, even though they do not have the law" (Romans 2: 14). In his treatise on law St. Thomas Aquinas comments, ". . . the light of natural reason, whereby we discern what is good and what is evil, which is the function of the natural law, is nothing else than an imprint on us of the Divine light." And C. S. Lewis writes, "The human mind has no more power of inventing a new value than of imagining a new primary color, or, indeed, of creating a new sun and a new sky for it to move in." Thus wisdom inherits, conserves, and transmits as old birds teach young birds how to fly. Lewis explains: "In a word, the old was a kind of propagation—men transmitting manhood to men: the new is merely propaganda."

The tradition of moral wisdom embodied in the perennial philosophy does not—like ideology—proceed from an intellectual or social elite to an ignorant, gullible, or unsophisticated populace. Fables, proverbs and folk tales originating in the ordinary life of common men reveal the same truths discovered by the moral sages. The fables of Aesop, classical myths, the folk tales of the Grimm brothers, and the traditional fairy tales of Hans Christian Andersen affirm the moral norms of the natural law and the perennial philosophy. For example, the fable "The Lion and the Mouse" teaches that a good deed is never wasted or lost; the myth "Baucis and Philemon" shows that wonderful things happen to ordinary people who practice hospitality to strangers with a pure, generous heart; the folk tale "The Frog Prince" illustrates that those who do kind favors, keep promises, and show humility see their dreams come true; the fairy tale "The Snow Queen" depicts the beauty and power of a child's innocence to melt hearts. All these stories reflect what C.S. Lewis in *The Abolition of Man*, citing Cicero, refers to as the law of general beneficence that underlies traditional morality: "Men were brought into existence for the sake of men that they might do one another good" (Cicero, *On Duties*). These simple stories, then, depict what Russell Kirk calls "the normative consciousness," the common sense understanding of right and wrong and sense and nonsense that the child pronounces when he utters "The king is naked!" Whereas ideology in its fanaticism scorns the natural and the normal and strives to invent "the thought that nobody ever had," the classics of children's literature and the great books embody "the thought that everybody has always had".

Unlike ideology's penchant for uniformity and homogeneity that Procrustes' rigidity represents, true wisdom transcends narrow-mindedness and closed systems. Whereas ideologies reduce reality to convenient categories and simplistic theories, the perennial philosophy embraces being in all its fullness and infinite variety. For Procrustes men can come in only one size and shape. In the perennial philosophy men come in all sizes and shapes. Ideologies abhor natural differences, hierarchical structures, and complex variations, but the perennial philosophy embraces God's plenty. In Chaucer's *The Canterbury Tales* all kinds of human beings form the Christian society that travels to the shrine of Thomas a` Becket: the ruling and noble class, the priesthood and the religious orders, and the craftsmen and laborers like the farmer, the carpenter, the miller, and the cook. This motley group contains variety within variety. Among the priestly class are saints and sinners ranging from the holy parson to the avaricious pardoner, and among the group of women are coy, sedate ladies with courtly manners like the Prioress and worldly, brazen women like the Wife of Bath. This merry company of medieval society embraces old and young, men and women, and the sophisticated and the vulgar, and it represents human nature in all of its four temperaments: melancholic, choleric, sanguine, and phlegmatic. However, within all this diversity dwells a fundamental unity. All the pilgrims relish a good story, delight in a hearty meal, enjoy the sociability of good conversation, and need the forgiveness of God's mercy. In short, *The Canterbury Tales* depicts human nature as both one and many, as predictable and surprising, and as noble and base. To use the philosopher Alan Watts' term, reality is "wiggly," not univocal.

Finally, the perennial philosophy conceives of the moral life as the fulfillment of duties rather than the assertion of rights. Religion means duty to God; piety means duty to parents, elders and ancestors; marriage means duty to one's husband or wife and obligations to children; and patriotism means duty to one's country. Virgil's "pious" Aeneas, the paragon of justice, duty, and service, subordinates his rights and his self-interest to his duties and the common good—the model of noble virtue. On the other hand, ideologies always elevate the rights of man (a euphemism for "self-interest") above moral duties—rights which seek liberation from moral law and from society's best interests. While the perennial philosophy distinguishes between the real and imaginary rights of man, its wisdom does not skew the balance between duties and rights. In Burke's words, all men have a right to justice:

They have a right to the fruits of their industry; and to the means of making their industry fruitful. They have a right to the acquisitions of their parents; to the nourishment and improvement of their offspring. . . . Whatever each man can separately do, without trespassing upon others, he has a right to do for himself; and he has a right to a fair portion of all which society, with all its combinations of skill and force, can do in his favor. In this partnership all men have equal rights; but not to equal things.

Ideology, however, ignores the condition which stipulates "without trespassing upon others" and demands, not true justice or equal rights, but "equal things". Feminist ideology that demands "the right to one's own body" trespasses upon the child's right to life. It demands "equal things" in its claim that no inherent, genetic differences except childbearing distinguish the proclivities and sensibilities of men and women. The false assumption that equal rights mean the right of homosexual couples to adopt children or marry trespasses upon the rights of children to a natural family. The homosexual lobby in its demand for same-sex marriage also seeks "equal things"—the social and economic benefits of marriage and the moral respectability of matrimony that normal marriages enjoy. Justice, however, is not quantitative or mathematical—a matter of equal things—but qualitative and proportionate: the duty to God is not the same as the duty to a parent or the duty to a spouse or the duty to a child. Society's duty to homosexual unions is not the same as its obligations to married couples, and society's duties to women urging reproductive rights is not the same as the state's obligation to protect innocent human life. Ideology in its obsession with rights denies this self-evident fact about the nature of justice and the reality of duty.

The perennial philosophy, then, is not just another ideology. It has passed the test of time, and it transcends every nation and culture. It respects the nature of things and the created order and does not twist reality. It honors the past and foresees the future, recalling its duties both to elders and to children. It trusts the accumulated wisdom of the entire world rather than the lucubrations of one intellectual, and it associates the moral life with the fulfillment of real duties rather than the expression of imaginary rights. And it contemplates the world in the light of the most universal and timeless truths instead of the intellectual fads of the day. To eliminate this body of knowledge taught in classical philosophy, the great books, and in the Catholic Church is to create an enormous void into which nothing can come from nothing.

Chapter 4. Consciousness and Unconsciousness in Orwell's *1984*

In his futuristic dystopia *1984* and in his essay "The Prevention of Literature," George Orwell demonstrates that totalitarian governments and ideological regimes censor, suppress or "prevent" bona fide literature in order to disseminate propaganda that advances a narrow political orthodoxy that stunts the full range of human consciousness in thought and feeling. As Orwell writes, in totalitarian societies, "Orthodoxy is unconsciousness." Thought control and thought police by means of the repetition of slogans and party lines on telescreens limit the range of human consciousness to the doctrinaire tenets of Big Brother. In the course of a typical day, the main character Winston Smith produces the lies of revisionist history at the Ministry of Truth, hears the fabricated news of Oceania's military victories on the telescreen, reads the advertisements promoting Victory gin and Victory cigarettes, and hears ad nauseam the catch-phrases "War is Peace," "Freedom Is Slavery," and "Ignorance Is Strength." Of course all this indoctrination intends to dull Winston's mind, deaden his conscience, and desensitize his emotions so that he is reduced to a mere creature of the state. The underlying psychology of Big Brother's propaganda machinery attempts to reduce Winston's awareness of reality to a total, uncritical acceptance of the government's official policies and beliefs even if that means affirming 2+2=5. Banned from Winston's consciousness are memories of his family and childhood, reminders of the beautiful craftsmanship and glorious art of the past, images of churches and worship, and a recollection of the great literature of Western civilization.

Whenever a society suffers "the prevention of literature," the human psyche ceases to experience the entire spectrum of human awareness—sensory, emotional, intellectual, or spiritual—that classical philosophers defined as *capax universi* (capable of the universe, able to understand universal truths). If "the soul is everything that is" by virtue of being *capax universi*, man's breadth of knowledge and feeling encompasses transcendental realities such as God, truth, goodness, and beauty and possesses depths of feeling that pierce the human heart in the moments of wonder, love, and death that expand human consciousness to rise above the humdrum routine of getting and spending. Describing his constant state of mind in *1984*, Winston laments the dismal joylessness of his daily life: "It struck him that the truly characteristic thing about modern life was not its cruelty and security, but simply its bareness, its dinginess, its listlessness." Winston enlarges his constricted consciousness only when he defies Big Brother and records his forbidden thoughts in his diary: "DOWN WITH BIG BROTHER." Winston's emotions awaken when he experiences the sexual attraction of Julia (a violation of state policy) and when he visits a pawn shop in the forbidden Prole district and marvels at the exquisite art displayed by an intricate paperweight, "a round, smooth thing that gleamed softly in the lamplight"—a moment of aesthetic pleasure that moves him to say "it's a beautiful thing." Another episode in the Prole district that heightens Winston's awareness and awakens a fond memory is the recognition of an engraving on a building once known as St. Clement's Dane—a name that recalls a childhood rhyme that he begins to hum: "oranges and lemons, say the bells of St. Clement's. . . ." These honest confessions in his diary, moments of wonder in the experience of the beautiful, and happy memories of the past—the quintessential moments of human experience—are banned by the "reality control" administered by Big Brother that attempts to impose a dehumanized consciousness upon all the members of the party. The highest compliment conferred upon a member of the party is "goodthinkful," a form of Newspeak with the definition "Meaning naturally orthodox, incapable of thinking a bad thought" as exemplified in Winston's deceased wife: "She had not a thought in her head . . ., and there was no imbecility, absolutely none, that she was not capable of swallowing if the party handed it out to her."

In this realm of Thought Control, the prevention of literature and the manipulation of language naturally follow: "The hunting-down and destruction of books had been done with the same thoroughness in the Prole quarters as everywhere else. It was very unlikely that there existed anywhere in Oceania a copy of a book printed earlier than 1960." Consequently, this ban on the great literature of the past stifles thought and flattens language: "Every year fewer and fewer words, and the range of consciousness always a little smaller." This prevention of old literature, as C. S. Lewis explained in his essay "On the Reading of Old Books," forms a narrow-mindedness and parochialism that breed a blindness to the universal and the timeless—a bias that only old books counteract. Lewis's rule—"after reading a new book, never to allow yourself another new one till you have read an old one"—recommends older literature because "We all, therefore, need the books that will correct the characteristic mistakes of our own period." Lewis refers to these great classics as the antidote to the biases that afflict a modern consciousness prejudiced by its snobbery: "The only palliative is to keep the clean sea breeze of the centuries blowing through our minds."

Without the expansive consciousness cultivated by the great literature of the past, then, the entire spectrum of human sensibility suffers as it acquires a dullness that desensitizes it to the heights and depths, the agony and ecstasy, of a human being's range of perception. Without the breadth of experience afforded by old classics, the human consciousness is not only half-alive or semi-awake but also loses touch with what Russell Kirk called "the normative consciousness." The old books also heighten the moral sense that sharply distinguishes between good and evil as Shakespeare's *Macbeth* demonstrates, between bad manners, good manners, and false manners as *Pride and Prejudice* illustrates, and between the civilized and the barbaric as the *Odyssey* illuminates—classics which establish the meaning of *human, moral,* and *normal* with no equivocation. This ability of great literature to encompass all the human emotions from the broken heart of Shakespeare's King Lear on the wild heath to the ecstasy of Dante ascending to the Beatific Vision enlarges the human understanding beyond the half-consciousness imposed by ideology. The power of the classics to engage all the intellectual faculties—memory, imagination, wonder—cultivates a sense of the universal, the perennial, the transcendent, and the normative that curb what Solzhenitsyn in his Harvard address of 1978, "A World Split Apart," calls "fashionable trends of thought" that produce "strong mass prejudices" that form a herd mentality. Thus without this hearty nourishment of the old books and "the healthy sea breezes of the centuries" to counteract ideology, intellectual trendiness, and the prejudices of the age, a void forms that is quickly filled by the media posing as oracles of wisdom.

Imagine a human mind digesting knowledge and information from only one source, the newspaper. In his address Solzhenitsyn censures the press for "deformation," disproportion," "guesswork, rumors, and suppositions to fill in the voids," "hasty, immature, superficial and misleading judgments," and he argues, "people have the right not to know," meaning "the right not to have their divine souls stuffed with gossip, nonsense, vain talk." The liberal bias of newspapers like *The Washington Post, New York Times*, and *The Boston Globe* that advocate and defend revolutionary ideas like abortion on demand, no- fault divorce, same-sex marriage, and militarism creates the illusion that all critics of these policies belong to a benighted minority of religious bigots, ring-wing extremists, and intolerant reactionaries. However, no great classics have extolled the slaughtering of the innocents, the blessings of divorce, new definitions of marriage, reinventions of femininity, or the abuse of military power. For example, Milton in *Paradise Lost* identifies the perversion of child sacrifice as the butchery of demons cast into hell:

> First Moloch, horrid king besmear'd with blood
> Of human sacrifice, and parents' tears,

Though for the noise of Drums and timbrels
loud
Their children's cries unheard, that past
through fire
To his grim Idol.

Homer's *Odyssey* celebrates the glory of traditional marriage and the greatness of womanhood in the devotion of Penelope to her husband and family: "The fame of her great virtue will never die. The immortal gods will lift a song in praise of self-possessed Penelope." Homer's *Iliad* depicts the brutal savagery of war as an uncontrollable madness unleashing the destructive forces of Strife, Panic, and Terror that destroy happy families and break the hearts of fathers, mothers, wives, and children. In the words of Hector's mother Hecuba, "O my child—my desolation! How can I go on living? What agonies must I suffer now, now you are dead and gone?" Without this knowledge of literature that forms the human heart and illuminates the normative consciousness, the abnormal, the unnatural, the immoral, and the inhuman become commonplace.

Imagine the human mind limited only to the reading of popular magazines. With the deluge of advertising that glamorizes fashions, markets the latest consumer products and highlights the feature articles that romanticize the idols of film and music, a media-influenced popular culture shapes the consciousness and cultivates a taste for the risqué, the novel, the trendy, and the sensationalistic. This popular culture produces in image after image an idea of happiness as the utopia of endless pleasurable sensations and an accumulation of the newest possessions. The graphic, colorful imagery and photography equate the art of living and the quest for adventure with romantic sensuality and the pursuit of the exotic. Popular culture forms an idea of human happiness as luxurious living, sophisticated style, and exotic travel. Without the images of happiness from old books to provide a standard of comparison, the human consciousness settles for the banal, the tawdry, and the mediocre. The average and the lowest common denominator become the norm instead of the excellent and the ideal.

For example, in Hans Andersen's "The Swineherd" the emperor's daughter rejects the prince's precious gift of a rare rose that blooms once in every five years, "a flower so sweet that whoever breathed its scent forgot all cares and sorrows." She also depreciates the prince's gift of a nightingale whose haunting melody produces the mystery of heavenly music. These two precious gifts, especially selected for the emperor's daughter by the prince as the most priceless tokens of his pure love, the best of its kind, find no favor with the emperor's daughter whose sense of taste fails to discriminate between the beautiful and the cheap, between the priceless and the worthless. When the noble prince disguises himself into a lowly swineherd and offers to sell the princess two odd novelties—a strange pot that detects the smells in the neighbors' kitchens and an odd rattle that produces the popular music of the day—she gladly pays the price of ten kisses and then one hundred kisses to a stranger for these trivial items. She prefers the common smells in the next door kitchen to the fragrance of the most perfect rose, and for the price of kisses paid to a stranger she will purchase the noises produced by the rattle rather than hear the heavenly music of the nightingale's song offered as a gift of love. Andersen depicts the princess's loss of the normative consciousness as she favors popular jigs and manufactured novelties to the music and beauty of heaven. In Andersen's story the standard of comparison exposes the world of difference between the sources of true happiness symbolized by the rose and the nightingale and the momentary thrills of a popular culture signified by the pot and the rattle—the latest fashion.

Imagine a human consciousness formed primarily by the pervasive influence of the film industry and the images of a video culture that gloats upon the violent, the vulgar, the sensationalistic, the lurid, and the pornographic. Then human consciousness soon comes to equate normalcy with the sights and sounds in the romances, adventures, and pseudo-heroic performances of the movie stars. In Walker Percy's *The Moviegoer* the main character Binx laments the "everydayness" of ordinary living that he associates with a stultifying boredom that only "the aura of heightened reality" in movies overcomes. He complains that his daily life is drab and perfunctory: "One bright texture of investments, family projects, lovely old houses, little theater readings and such. It comes over me: this is how one lives." This addiction to movie-going leads a person to seek escapes from reality, to inhabit a private world divorced from human relationships and associations, and to pursue diversions to relieve the burden of time. As Binx confesses, "For years now I have had no friends. I spend my entire time working, making money, going to movies, and seeking the company of women." Binx's human consciousness has atrophied to the point that nothing is urgent. Despite his aunt's protests that a thirty year old man should follow a vocation, have aspirations, go to medical school, and contribute to the common good, Binx's only reaction is "What's wrong with this? All I have to do is remember it." Then he cynically adds, "I will say yes though I do not know what she is talking about." A moviegoer, not a reader, Binx demonstrates a passive indifference to the normal pursuits of career, romance, family, and the future that signify an alienation from the primary realities of normative experience. Thus Walker Percy depicts the deadening effects of a lifetime of films upon the consciousness of the moviegoer who acts half-alive and emotionally unresponsive.

On the other hand, the great folk literature of the West embodied in the *Household Stories* of the Grimm brothers and the fairy tales of Hans Andersen recall the perennial truth that wonderful things happen to ordinary people living in a family, doing their daily chores, cooking and cleaning the house, or going to the market. Whether it is simple Hans finding great luck ("There is no man under the sun who is so fortunate as I am"), the humble Cinderella discovering the miraculous joy of love ("the king's son danced with her only, and if any one invited her to dance, he said: 'This is my partner'."), or the lively Tom Thumb bringing mirth into the home ("How sad it is we have no children," the wife lamented; "even if we had only one, and it were quite small, and only as big as a thumb . . . we would still love it with all our hearts"), these old tales present a vision of normal life that transcends the dreary "everydayness" that oppresses Binx in his daily regimen. These tales of domestic life in the modest circumstances of common life depict the wonders of dreams coming true, surprises of great good fortune, and miracles of beauty and goodness interwoven in the business of everyday living. Folktales restore human perception to a normative consciousness that senses mysteries, paradoxes, luck, goodness, beauty, and Divine Providence in the humble circumstances of simple living—a vision alien to the Hollywood film industry.

Imagine a mind formed by the indoctrination of liberal ideologies in the politically correct world of public schools and American higher education. In these places the "prevention" of bona fide literature means the politicization of English and Humanities departments that reduce the classics to deconstruction, to "Eurocentric" bias, to "dead white man's literature," to a study of literature as cultural studies—a view of literature as the politics of race, class, gender, and minorities. Multicultural literature, feminist literature, and the literature of homosexuality derange the entire Western canon as these subjects compromise great literature's sense of the transcendent and reduce the humanities to the political agendas manipulating educational institutions to pander to intellectual fashions that attack the classical-Christian notions of the moral, the normal, and the traditional. Instead of the literature that qualifies as "the best that has been thought and said" (Matthew Arnold), as books that inspire human beings "to enable the readers better to enjoy life, or better to endure it" (Samuel Johnson), as great books that capture the unchanging nature of the human heart (C.S. Lewis), modern educational curricula commit the fault that Dr. Johnson in *Rasselas* identified as numbering "the streaks of the tulip"—the microscopic examination of accidental features, insignificant particularities, and minor details with no comprehension of the work of art as a whole.

Great literature like the *Odyssey*, on the other hand, affirms timeless universal truths that remain the same in all times, places, and cultures. In Homer's classic the family is the source of civilization, the strength of the family depends on the fidelity of a husband and wife in the indissoluble union of marriage, the purpose of civilized life is to be productive and fruitful both in the field and in the family, and happiness is the reward of beholding the harvest of family life in the form of children and grandchildren in the same spirit of gratitude that one marvels at the bounty of the orchards. Great literature like Jane Austen's *Pride and Prejudice* affirms the nobility and dignity of marriage when men and women marry for the purest reasons of love and esteem for one another—not money, respectability, or pleasure—and when they fall in love with their entire being of mind, heart, and conscience and not for the economic reasons of a "proper match" or for the social motive of escaping the stigma of old maid. Great literature is not preoccupied with the politics of race, culture, sex, or class but interested in the universal experiences of war, love, death, suffering, and happiness. Homer's *Iliad* presents the human condition both when barbarism prevails and war's brutal violence destroys civilization and families and when civilization flourishes and the art of living well brings prosperity, fruitfulness, leisure, and the fine arts into a country. Cervantes' *Don Quixote* depicts the human condition as vulgar or coarse when an age lacks the virtues of knight-errantry—truth, honor, courtesy, chivalry, courage—and degenerates to the base world of the Iron Age where money and utility determine all human relationships, and the novel demonstrates the human condition as beautiful when noble men honor their oaths, serve women, and live for the highest ideals as they strive to restore the Golden Age. Shakespeare's

King Lear presents the human condition when the love of power and ambition reduce life to an animal kingdom where might is right and "man's life's as cheap as beast's," and it portrays the human condition when the filial bonds of affection and the faithful devotion of friendship cultivate kindness and gratitude that redeems the world.

In short, human consciousness can be shrunk or expanded, debilitated or animated. If limited to the mental stimulation of newspapers, magazines, movies, and ideological education, man's potential to be *capax universi* shrivels as he suffers the various techniques of mind control and indoctrination that replace honest thinking with political clichés, the love of truth with political ideologies, and the passionate life of the mind with mental apathy. Instead of fearlessly declaring 2+2=4 or "the king is naked," ideological man furnishes the mind with its daily ration of the media whose effect resembles the tranquilizing drug "soma" in Aldous Huxley's *Brave New World*—the drug that prevents the depths of emotion that fill the heart and touch the soul and suppresses passion, courage, anger, heroism, and restlessness. Instead of real sentiments and honest emotions the state of unconsciousness repeats slogans like "I'm ok, you're ok," slogans about being "tolerant" and non-judgmental and about "diversity." "I'd rather watch a movie than read a book." "We're living together." "I'm pro-choice." These responses are the politically correct responses that correspond with the reactions produced by soma: "Let's go on a soma holiday." In this passive mental apathy where human beings depend on an exclusive knowledge class to do their thinking and to determine intellectual fashions with the power of the media, the condition is ripe for the easy establishment of nonsense, lies, and propaganda as enlightened wisdom and progressive thinking.

Only in this state where "orthodoxy is unconsciousness" in a politically correct world does man in his stupor close his conscience just as he deadens his mind and hardens his heart to self-evident truths. How can a person's conscience be so dead as to will, legislate, or perform the killing of babies under the pretext of a woman's right to control her body? How can a person's mind be so brainwashed as to miss the obvious purpose and meaning of marriage as intended by Mother Nature and as designed by Divine Providence? How can human sensibility be so desensitized as to assume that cohabitation expresses love and means the same as marriage? How can man's common sense be so deranged as to deny the obvious nature of maleness and femaleness and invent terms like bisexual and transgendered? Only in an Orwellian universe can one deny that water is wet, rocks are hard, and 2+2=4 and then reinvent reality to proclaim "War is Peace" or, in the words of Satan in *Paradise Lost*, "Evil, be thou my good." There is no normative consciousness, no human sensibility, no right reason, and no voice of conscience in a culture where old books have no educational influence to enlarge human knowledge by comparing the present to the past. By distinguishing between the way things are to the way things ought to be, by judging human actions by divine law, by discerning the distinction between the civilized and the barbaric, and by distinguishing between the natural and the unnatural, the norm becomes self-evident.

Modernity has lost its sense of a human consciousness. Lacking this moral sensibility, it shows no mercy for babies killed in abortion, no pity for children subjected to the cruelty of divorce or adopted in disordered same-sex unions, and no compassion for children robbed of their innocence in Planned Parenthood's aggressive sex education agenda. The stunted consciousness engendered by political orthodoxy and the media reveals insensibility to human refinement, delicacy, and tact as evidenced by the bad taste of advertisements on television, by the sexually explicit nature of Hollywood films, and by the obscenities that abound in films with "R" ratings. The normative consciousness needs restoration through bona fide education that respects the wisdom of the past, teaches old books as repositories of perennial truths, and illuminates the profound differences between the sentiments of a civilized human being and the savagery of a Cyclops, between the meaning of marital love and the promiscuity of lust, between the conscience of a person endowed with the natural moral law and the hardheartedness of rulers who view human life with contempt. Without Shakespeare's *Macbeth* presenting in stark honesty the horror of cold-blooded murder, the tortured mind of the guilty, and the unnaturalness of Lady Macbeth proclaiming "Unsex me," the half-alive consciousness will rationalize evil. Without Homer's *Iliad* portraying the tragedy of fathers, husbands, and sons dying in war with their houses "half-built," mothers and wives grieving with broken hearts at the destruction of their homes and marriages, vainglorious political leaders will precipitate nations into unjust wars in the name of abstractions that hide the hideousness of war's dehumanizing cruelty. Without Austen's *Pride and Prejudice* depicting the false ideas of marriage motivated by social prestige, economic security, or lustful attraction and upholding the noble ideal of marriage as mutual esteem, deep affection, natural attraction, and admiration of each other's moral character, then marriage loses its status as a holy, venerable institution that provides life its richest source of contentment. George Orwell, prophetic seer, foresaw the grave consequences to civilization when he observed "the prevention of literature" and imagined an intellectually, emotionally, morally starved world without old books that would, in C.S. Lewis's words, "keep the clean sea breezes of the centuries blowing through our minds."

Chapter 5. The Wisdom of the World and the Wisdom of God

The wisdom of the world always poses as realism, as the sure way to succeed, prosper, and win. It wears the mask of superior intelligence and irrefutable logic and gives the impression of level-headedness and blunt honesty. It regards itself as the antidote to quixotic fantasies and naive religious ideals which do not correspond to the hard truths of the world as it is and to the real facts of human nature. Polonius's famous advice to Laertes in *Hamlet* illustrates one form of this worldly wisdom which considers itself infallible. In a series of warnings that counsel artfulness and duplicity, Polonius encourages his son in the practice of cunning and plotting: "Give thy thoughts no tongue," "Be thou familiar, but by no means vulgar," "But do not dull thy palm with entertainment" [hospitality], "Beware of entrance to a quarrel," "Give every man thy ear but few thy voice," "Neither a borrower nor lender be." Polonius's politic advice to his son consists of precautions about speaking the truth, about being generous in the treatment of others, about revealing passionate convictions, and about forming close relationships. The advice is negative: watch out, be careful, take no chances, be on guard, trust no one, hide what you think. Worldly wisdom dictates neutrality or "moderation" in the sense of lukewarm, being neither hot nor cold. Life is a chess game, and therefore one must always be on the defensive and be more cunning and calculating than the opposition. Exaggerating man's foreknowledge and discounting the mystery of Divine Providence, worldly wisdom holds that man alone determines the outcome of events. Worldly wisdom, despite all its claims to higher knowledge and dark secrets that lead to victory, amounts to false prudence—the pretense of foreknowledge— as Polonius's example testifies. The advisor to King Claudius who claims to know the cause of Hamlet's presumed madness (unrequited love) has no idea of the real truth (Hamlet's suspicion of Claudius as the murderer of his father). The spy who imagines himself privy to state secrets is accidentally killed when hiding behind the curtains eavesdropping on Hamlet and his daughter Ophelia.

Machiavelli in *The Prince* also defends worldly wisdom as the source of political power, arguing that only the appearance of goodness—not real moral integrity— is required for the success of rulers:

> It is good to appear merciful, truthful, humane, sincere, and religious; it is good to be so in reality. But you must keep your mind so disposed that, in case of need, you can turn to the exact contrary. This has to be understood: a prince, and especially a new prince, cannot possibly exercise all those virtues for which men are called 'good.' To preserve the state, he often has to do things against his word, against charity, against humanity, against religion.

As Machiavelli explains, public image matters more than moral character because "the masses are always impressed by the superficial appearance of things. . . . And the world consists of nothing but the masses." Thus cleverness in deceiving others and artfulness in concealing one's intentions become the virtues instilled by worldly wisdom. Moral absolutes, religious norms, and noble ideals play no part in the way of the world which requires men to imitate the fox or the lion. For Machiavellian politicians goodness is all form and no substance. When Polonius advised his son, "To thine own self be true," he did not counsel self knowledge or the courage of conviction but the rule of self-interest. Man is the measure of all things, the one who determines right and wrong according to the standards of expediency, utilitarianism, and "situation ethics". If victory is achieved and the prince gains power, then the end justifies the means. Because Hannibal's "inhuman cruelty" prevented the rebellion of his forces and Scipio's "excessive leniency" led to the revolt of his armies in Spain, Machiavelli equates the moral way with naïve folly and the worldly way with practical wisdom. Worldly wisdom gives no credence to the first principle of Christian wisdom: "But seek first his kingdom and his righteousness, and all these things shall be yours as well" (Matthew 6: 33).

The guiles of worldly wisdom continue to lure modern man in many subtle ways. To run for president in the United States, political expediency dictates that a candidate equivocate in the wily manner recommended by Polonius or deceive the masses with superficial appearances posing as absolute truth. As Machiavelli would say, it is good to decry abortion, war, and taxes, but to win elections one may have to abandon moral principles and make concessions to the masses or to the party line or to the political lobbies that provide the greatest contributions. Regardless of how extreme, radical, or immoral the positions politicians espouse, they must appear good, "moderate," or tolerant to the masses and to the media, that is, politically correct. Thus Catholic politicians who compromise the moral teachings of the Church about the intrinsic evils of contraception, abortion, embryonic stem cell research, and same-sex marriage follow the counsel of Polonius and Machiavelli. Guided by the motives of self-interest, safety, security, and re-election, they take no political risks and pronounce no moral convictions besides the lame, neutral position of "I am personally opposed to abortion but . . ." or "If I had only known then what I know now"—the essence of Polonius's circumspect advice. Polonius would advise a pro-life politician to keep his thoughts to himself ("Give thy thoughts no tongue"), and Machiavelli would counsel a politician opposed to the Iraq War to abandon his scruples: a prince "should not depart from the good if he can hold to it, but he should be ready to enter on evil if he has to." Worldly wisdom is the art of changing course and varying one's political and moral views to suit the spirit of the times, to pander to the masses, or to gain political advantages for the sake of self-interest. As Machiavelli explains, the prince "has to have a mind ready to shift as the winds of fortune and the varying circumstances of life may dictate." In short, worldly wisdom never exalts truth, justice, God, or the common good above political ideology and the will to power.

In the realm of family life, worldly wisdom encourages two incomes and a small family as the "safe," risk-free normative American and European way of life. Because Polonius's watchword is "Beware," his philosophy inhibits the generosity of love, the nobility of friendship, the romance of adventure, and chivalric liberality. The purposes of self-interest and economic prosperity ("To thine own self be true") demand extreme carefulness, not an abandonment to Divine Providence. Riddled with anxiety and trepidation, worldly wisdom advocates contraception and abortion as necessary forms of man-made control to eliminate the chance of undesirable or unpredictable births. Caution, fear, and prevention, the watchwords of Polonius who exhorts his son always to be wary and guarded, govern the policies of worldly wisdom. Devious and roundabout, worldly wisdom does not honor sacred oaths or uphold indissoluble vows, imagining that winning at all costs dictates sacrificing moral principles to accomplish self-serving purposes. Cloning, embryonic stem-cell research, and permissive no fault divorce laws all follow the indirect, crooked path to an end that Machiavelli prescribed, the twisted notion that one can do evil to achieve good. They all violate the sense of the sacred or the sanctity of a vow—dishonoring the dignity of human life or denigrating the honor of a promise. These habits and mores all derive from the spirit of Polonius's philosophy that avoids any passionate commitment to an absolute moral standard ("Beware of entrance to a quarrel"), and they correspond to Machiavelli's mockery of simplistic idealism: "Any man who tries to be good all the time is bound to come to ruin among the great number who are not good." The worldly wise assume that man is a powerful, all-knowing god with the sovereign freedom to do as he wishes—dictate democracy, invade nations, kill babies, redefine marriage, and reinvent morality. Worldly wisdom never thinks in terms of self-sacrifice, the gift of self, the virtue of magnanimity, or the fidelity to promises.

In the field of education worldly wisdom advocates the contemporary version of "To thine own self be true". Indoctrinating young minds to Planned Parenthood's view of human sexuality as recreational entertainment, worldly wisdom instills in the young the rule of self indulgence and instant gratification. The pleasurable is the good. Perpetuating the myths of diversity and tolerance as the epitome of moral excellence, public education panders to the lowest common denominator and appeals to the "masses" that Machiavelli identified as the powerful influence of the world. Secular public education offers to students a version of the philosophy of Polonius: Follow the crowd, blend in, stay neutral, be politically correct, act trendy, do not be judgmental. Just as Polonius counsels moral neutrality in advising his son "Neither a borrower nor a lender be," the worldly wisdom that prevails in modern education also teaches moral indifference in the form of relativism. Right and wrong are cultural and variable and have no universal meaning. No noble cause inspires a passionate love of goodness, and no unspeakable evil evokes a sense of loathing at the ugliness of sin. On the university level, worldly wisdom counsels political correctness, the obsession with never offending anyone with moral objections or speaking one's mind in words that might be construed as "hate speech". In the typical atmosphere of many liberal colleges, one must walk a tightrope and literally "Give thy thoughts no tongue" and "Beware of entrance to a quarrel" lest he suffer accusations of sexism, racism, Eurocentrism, anti-Semitism, or homophobia. Whether it is being "safe" by way of contraception and abortion on demand or "politically correct" by way of silence and intimidation, worldly wisdom operates by means of cowardice and fearfulness and is dominated by a compulsion for security. Moral neutrality, self-interest, artful duplicity, and circumspect wariness summarize the traits of worldly wisdom. In Hans Andersen's "The Emperor's New Clothes," no members of the court dared to tell the king he was naked because they feared losing their privileged position, the many perquisites of royal favor, and the image of respectability; they all lacked the child's spontaneous truthfulness in uttering the simple truth: "He's nothing on!"

Christian wisdom, on the other hand, does not require clever deviousness, elaborate pretending, or labyrinthine scheming. The teaching "But seek first his kingdom and his righteousness, and all these things shall be yours as well" surpasses Polonius's negative warnings about being careful, cautious, skeptical, and suspicious. Christian wisdom distinguishes between what C.S Lewis calls "first things" and "second things". Explaining that a woman who makes a dog the first priority in her life "loses, in the end, not only her human usefulness and dignity but even the proper pleasure of dog-keeping" and that a man who equates the whole meaning of the universe to his passion for one woman also loses the full experience of human love, Lewis clarifies this basic truth of Christian moral wisdom:

> Every preference of a small good to a great,
> or a partial good to a total good, involves the
> loss of the small or partial good for which

the sacrifice was made. If Esau really got his mess of pottage in return for his birthright, then Esau was a lucky exception. You can't get second things by putting them first; you can get second things only by putting first things first.

If the fear of the Lord is the beginning of wisdom, if the first of the Ten Commandments is "I am the Lord your God: you shall not have strange gods before me," and if the first of the two great commandments is "You shall love the Lord your God with all your heart, and with all your soul, and with all your mind, and with all your strength," then Christian wisdom puts first things first. If the invasion of Iraq fails to satisfy all the conditions for a just war, then truth and justice supersede loyalty to a political party or ideology. If God enjoins, "Be fruitful and multiply" and Christ says of divorce, "It was not so from the beginning," then these holy words bind the human conscience more than all the propaganda of Planned Parenthood and all the feminist politics of reproductive rights. If the Church teaches that abortion is always intrinsically evil and that homosexuality is disordered and sinful, then the moral law surpasses the policies of the United Nations and the decisions of courts that legalize evil and allow same-sex marriage. If Christ teaches, "What doth it profit a man to gain the whole world and lose his soul," then no amount of wealth, pleasure, fame, or power can compensate for a guilty conscience and an immoral life. Because it puts first things first and second things second, Christian wisdom escapes the lies and delusions of worldly wisdom that promise everything but deliver nothing. The Iraq War has not delivered an oppressed people or spread democracy but provoked civil war and increased terrorism. The contraceptive mentality has not relieved the conflicts of marriage or produced the emancipation of women but has increased divorce, spread sexually transmitted diseases, and produced the childlessness that Patrick Buchanan called "the Death of the West" in his book by that name. Christian wisdom begins when man heeds the words of Mary to the servants at the marriage of Cana: "Do whatever he tells you"—not what the masses, the political parties, or the courts tell you.

Christian wisdom teaches the purity of truthfulness and shuns the artfulness and cunning of worldly wisdom. As Christ enjoined his disciples, "Let your answer be 'yes, yes, no, no.' " To inherit the kingdom of God man must imitate a child in his candor and reject guile in all its subtle forms: "Truly, I say to you, unless you turn and become like little children, you will never enter the kingdom of heaven" (Matthew 18: 3). Like the child in Hans Andersen's "The Emperor's New Clothes," man must not be intimidated by popular public opinion fashioned by the weavers who spin their lies for their own gain and threaten dissenters with the stigma of being incompetent or stupid. While worldly wisdom thrives on sophistry, jargon, euphemism, and Orwellian Newspeak, Christian wisdom speaks in the eloquence of the simple truth. Life begins at conception and does not depend on the "penumbras" and emanations of the Constitution. Partial birth abortion is infanticide, not a woman's reproductive right. "Male and female he created them" and "Therefore a man leaves his mother and father and cleaves to his wife, and they become one flesh." There is no such thing as same-sex marriage under "the equal protection of the law." Worldly wisdom obfuscates the simplest and most self-evident truths with tortured logic, specious reasoning, and verbal engineering that resemble Orwell's Newspeak: War is Peace, Ignorance is Strength, Freedom is Slavery. The contemporary version of those statements from *1984* is Unjust War is Just War, Lying is Truth, Sickness is Health, and Female is Male. Christian wisdom, on the other hand, clarifies moral truths with perfect luminosity that dispels all doubts and ambiguities: The beatitude "Blessed are the pure in heart, for they shall see God" honors those with clear minds, clean consciences, and truthful words who never equivocate. As Winston said in *1984*, "Stones are hard, water is wet, objects unsupported fall toward the earth's center." When a person says yes to the truth and no to the lie, he is agreeing that the king is naked. Like Winston who insists that 2+2 is 4 and that "being in a minority, even a minority of one, did not make you mad," Christian wisdom does not pretend that the king looks resplendent even though the weavers, the ministers of government, court officials, and the populace all flatter the king with compliments like "it's magnificent".

Christian wisdom does not counsel the paranoid fear and excessive caution of Polonius or the wiliness of the fox that Machiavelli recommends. It teaches confidence in God, trust in Divine Providence, and belief in the Father's love. The Sermon on the Mount exhorts man, "Do not be anxious about your life" and discourages useless worry about the future. Reminding the world of the Divine Providence of God, Christ explains, "Look at the birds in the air of the air: they neither sow nor reap nor gather into barns, and yet your heavenly Father feeds them." When the disciples saw Christ walking on the water and felt terrified as they imagined a ghost, again they learned the foolishness of irrational fear: "Take heart, it is I; have no fear." Peter too was reprimanded when he walked on the water but lost courage when he heard the wind: "O man of little faith, why did you doubt?" The hysteria about overpopulation publicized in the 1970s in books like Paul Ehrlich's *The Population Bomb* and the nervousness about unexpected pregnancies that haunts families which contraceptively limit family size illustrates worldly wisdom governed by fear and lack of faith. The mentality of panic aroused by mention of weapons of mass destruction or "the axis of evil" that provokes preventive wars and aggressive invasions also proceeds from the same state of anxiety that trusts only human cunning and political calculation. Christian wisdom, on the other hand, teaches the cardinal virtue of prudence—foresight on behalf of others and future generations—rather than shrewd calculation or political craftiness for the sake of self-interest. Christian wisdom combines the wisdom of the serpent and the gentleness of the dove as it foresees consequences and prepares for the future with practical reason. As the parable of the wise virgins illustrates, the ten who remembered to bring the oil to light their lamps beheld the bridegroom while the foolish maidens were too late for the marriage feast. In making prudent choices, however, Christian wisdom avoids what Joseph Pieper in *The Four Cardinal Virtues* calls "desperate self-preservation, overriding concern for confirmation and security" and "the insidiousness, guile, craft, and concupiscence . . . of small-minded and small-souled persons." The prudence of Christian wisdom, on the other hand, is bold and adventurous, not cowardly or calculating, and transcends the narrow thinking of "Neither a borrower nor a lender be". The Beatitudes, a summary of Christian wisdom, teach noble action and moral heroism. Being pure, meek, merciful, and peacemaking demands more moral valor than being careful, reserved, and circumspect. Hungering and thirsting for righteousness and suffering persecution for righteous' sake demand more self-sacrifice and heroism than hiding behind a curtain or acting like a fox. As Pieper explains, true prudence reveals "the clear-eyed virtue of magnanimity" and "the constant readiness to ignore the self".

In short, worldly wisdom with its wariness, artfulness, and self-interest imagines victory and success in its view of life as a chess game, but its cunning results in defeat and suffering because it does not account for chance, surprise, or Divine Providence. Living for the moment and worshipping Mammon, it never considers eternity or the four last things. In its love of power, money, pleasure, or self, worldly wisdom gains the world but loses the soul. Worldly wisdom, then, is not prudence at all but fantasy and folly because it leads to lies, death, war, injustice, and godlessness. Christian wisdom, putting first things first, saying "Yes, yes" and No, no" without equivocation, and trusting in God's Providence with faith and confidence, leads to truth, peace, charity, and the Church—the highest things. Worldly wisdom produces the genocide of war, the culture of death, and the sterility of contraception and same-sex marriage. Christian wisdom, however, produces true happiness, the civilization of love, and the beatitude of eternal life, offering "the kingdom of heaven" to the poor of spirit and those persecuted for God's sake, the inheritance of the earth to the meek, and the vision of God for the pure in heart. By putting worldly wisdom first and God's wisdom second, modernity proves once again the moral truth that C.S. Lewis formulated: "You can't get second things by putting them first; you get second things only by putting first things first." By putting a nation's political ambitions before the Church's teaching about just war law, by exaggerating the woman's right to choice before the child's right to life, by elevating man's definition of same-sex marriage above God's teaching about the sacramental union of man and woman, and by idolizing ideology above Christian and human wisdom, modern man sacrifices his noble birthright for a mess of pottage—the anarchy of war, the death of the West, the destruction of the family, and the moral chaos of relativism.

Chapter 6. The Virtues of the Heart: The Mark of Civilization

Homer's *Odyssey* distinguishes between the civilized and the barbaric, between those who live *well* and those who merely live in the sense of mere animal survival, between those who live in hospitable, beautiful homes like Penelope, Menelaus, and Nestor and those who live in dark caves like the savage Cyclops. While the civilized delight in the fine arts, enjoy athletic contests and leisure, value knowledge, and cultivate the practical arts like shipbuilding, agriculture, and weaving, the barbarians like the Cyclops and the Suitors lack an appreciation of beauty, play, and the life of the mind. When Odysseus sojourns in the land of Phaeacia, he lives *well* because he is welcomed into a society that lives in peace, works for the common good, honors the gods, and respects the rule of law. The civilized not only work industriously but also cultivate leisure and play, enjoying the many fruits of civilization: feasts and banquets, music and dance, poetry and conversation, games and athletics. This human, balanced way of life originates in the home, the center of civilization—the place that refines and sensitizes the heart to the good, the true, and the beautiful. The modern world's notions of morality—while dictated by legal decisions, political ideologies, fashionable opinion, and utilitarianism—are not informed by the virtues of the heart: hospitality, loyalty, tenderness, purity, gratitude, and an appreciation of beauty.

All the civilized practice the virtue of hospitality and welcome travelers and strangers as if they were gods in disguise, a common occurrence in Greek literature. This virtue of the heart pities the lonely wanderings and homelessness of the traveler in dire need of food, sleep, comfort, and protection from enemies or the elements. As Menelaus explains in his welcome of Telemachus, "Just think of all the hospitality *we* enjoyed at the hands of other men before we made it home, and god save us from such hard treks in years to come." Penelope, offended by the vulgar insults and despicable treatment of the beggar in disguise in her palace, complains to her son, "Consider the dreadful thing just done in our halls—how you let the stranger be so abused." Penelope also reminds her maids, "Every stranger and beggar comes from Zeus, and whatever scrap we give him he'll be glad to get" as she insists on this virtue of kindness toward travelers. Telemachus, noticing the stranger Mentes (Pallas Athene in disguise) at the gate, immediately welcomes the guest: "Greetings, stranger! Here in our house you'll find a royal welcome. Have supper first, then tell us what you need." This old-world virtue of hospitality reveals the refined manners and sensitive heart learned in the home—a custom that cares for all the human needs of the guest— physical and emotional—as he is bathed and anointed, welcomed with the best food and wine, entertained with music or poetry, encouraged to narrate his adventures, and honored with gifts.

Loyalty marks another virtue of the heart learned in the culture of the home and practiced by the civilized. Odysseus's heroic struggles to return home to Ithaca and Penelope's fidelity to her husband during his twenty-year absence of course epitomize this loyalty of husband

and wife in marriage. Loyalty to parents and loyalty to children also reveal the deep bonds that unite family members in the course of a lifetime. Before Odysseus left for the Trojan War, he urged Penelope, "Watch over my father and mother in the palace, just as now, or perhaps a little more, when I am far from home." The swineherd Eumaeus, "that fine loyal man who of all the household hands of Odysseus ever had cared the most for his master's good"—even after twenty years of Odysseus's absence—continues to care for his master's herds and flocks with steadfast constancy, never wavering in his sense of duty and faithfulness because of his indebtedness to Odysseus's generous heart: "Never another master kind as he! I'll never find one—no matter where I go . . . so deeply he loved me, cared for me, so deeply." When Odysseus visits the underworld and converses with the spirits of the dead, he experiences the undying loyalty of family members in the indissolubility of love. In Hades, Anticleia, Odysseus' mother, laments, "No, it was longing for you, my shining Odysseus,—you and your quickness, you and your gentle ways—that tore away my life that had been sweet." Odysseus, in turn, implores his mother for news of his father, wife, and son to whom he is bonded forever despite their separation: "Tell me of father, tell of the son I left behind. . . . Please tell me about my wife. . . ." The great Achilles also feels profoundly his family ties to his son and father and yearns to be reunited with his loved ones: "But come, tell me the news about my gallant son. . . . Tell me of noble Peleus, any word you've heard." Thus in the culture of the home the loyalty of husband and wife, the bond of mother and child, the affection of father and son demonstrate the lifelong obligations or profound indebtedness that family members feel for one another from the depths of their hearts. Civilization cultivates true, loyal hearts.

This cultivation of the kind, generous, and loyal heart that the home and family engender also expresses itself in the form of tenderness, especially toward the young and the elderly. Odysseus fondly remembers the occasion when he visited his grandparents and participated in the sport of hunting with his grandfather: "His mother's mother, Amphithea, hugged the boy and kissed his face and kissed his shining eyes " as his uncles greet him warmly and shower him with handclasps. The grandfather and uncles cherish the young Odysseus as the apple of their eye as they prepare a great feast to welcome the child with festive joy. Eurycleia, Penelope's loyal maid—"the one of all the maids who loved the prince the most—she'd nursed him as a baby"— remembers nursing Odysseus's hunting wound during his visit to the grandparents. When she discovers his identity as the beggar in disguise, she utters with tears in her eyes, "Yes, yes! You are Odysseus—oh dear boy. . . ." This touching tenderness toward the young extends to the elderly. When Odysseus learns about the misery of his aged father Laertes from his mother in Hades, he yearns to care for him in his loneliness: " and there he lies in anguish . . . with his old age hard upon him, too, and his grief grows as he longs for your return." Achilles too in the underworld feels great sorrow about his inability to comfort his aging father, worrying "do they despise the man in Hellas and in Phthia because old age has lamed his arms and legs?" The glorious hero's deepest longing is "to help my father as once I helped our armies" and "Oh to arrive at my father's house—the man I was, for one brief day." The home cultivates this sense of tender loving care for the young and the elderly and affords them all the affection that life at its most delicate and vulnerable demands.

The atmosphere of the home that creates civilization also creates the pure heart and the virtue of modesty. When Odysseus arrives as a shipwrecked traveler in the land of Phaeacia, he first beholds the beautiful princess Nausicaa and apologizes for his disheveled, naked condition as he appeals to her kindness and respects her modesty: "Show me the way to town, give me a rag for cover." As he cleans his body and anoints it with oil, Odysseus avoids giving shame or scandal to Nausicaa and her maids: "But I won't bathe in front of you. I would be embarrassed—stark naked before young girls with lovely braids." As Odysseus follows Nausicaa to Phaeacia, Nausicaa's modesty forbids her from entering the town followed by the stranger lest "one of the coarser sort, spying us, might say, 'Now who's that tall, handsome stranger Nausicaa has in tow? . . . Her husband to be, just wait!'" To prevent gossip and slander, she urges Odysseus to wait in the grove until she reaches her father's palace so no rumors will spread about a maiden "consorting with men before she'd tied the knot in public." In this scene Odysseus approaches Nausicaa with the utmost tact and respects her maidenhood, and Nausicaa conducts herself with the utmost propriety and dignity—both man and woman sensitive about violating modesty and causing shame. Penelope likewise reflects these refined manners and high regard for the virtues of modesty and chastity—civilized ideals in her home which are violated by the promiscuity of the Suitors and their consorts: "I'd rather die, yes, better that by far than have to look on at your outrage day by day: guests treated to blows, men dragging serving-women through our noble house, exploiting them all, no shame!" The feminine sensibility of Nausicaa and Penelope that upholds the ideals of modesty, chastity, and purity evinces disgust at promiscuous sexuality and shameless lust. This virtue of the pure heart also grows in the culture of the family.

Gratitude is another virtue of the heart which the home instills. The civilized always pour libations to the gods before festive banquets; they always feel the obligation to repay their parents for their loving care. Servants and maids who are loyal to Laertes, Odysseus, Penelope, and Telemachus feel a lifelong gratitude because their debts to their masters are unrepayable. When they were uprooted, homeless, wandering, sold by pirates, or starving, they were welcomed into hospitable homes and civilized societies—"this gracious house so filled with the best that life can offer" as Penelope says—that allowed them to live a human life instead of the lot of the slave or exile. After being kidnapped by Phoenicians and sold by pirates, Eumaeus suffered the wretched life of a tramp when "at last, the wind and current bore us on to Ithaca, here where Laertes bought me with his wealth. And so I laid my eyes on this good land." Ever thankful for this gift of a sense of belonging to a home and to a law-abiding, God-fearing society, Eumaeus offers a lifetime of loyal service to his master's family: "Never another master kind as he! I'll never find one—no matter where I go. . . ." Eurycleia too was purchased by Laertes who paid a handsome price for the faithful servant and devoted nurse, and as grateful repayment she spent a lifetime loving all the members of the family who adopted her. The generous, hospitable hearts of loving fathers and mothers and the kind, compassionate hearts of rulers and masters nurture this virtue of the grateful heart as another fruit of the culture of the family.

The environment of the family also awakens a love of the beautiful and develops a sensitivity for aesthetic pleasures. Wherever hospitable homes with loving kindness flourish in the *Odyssey*, the atmosphere communicates beauty, and the refined heart is touched by the beauty of the natural world, appreciates the fine arts of music, dance, and poetry, wonders in awe at the miracles of beautiful craftsmanship, or marvels at the beauty of the human form. When Homer describes a festive banquet or a simple welcome in homes, the atmosphere of formality and elegance always radiates beauty: "A maid brought water soon in a graceful golden pitcher and over a silver basin tipped it out so they might rinse their hands, and then pulled a gleaming table to their side." When Telemachus enters Menelaus's palace, he exclaims "My eyes dazzle . . . I am struck with wonder" as he beholds the king's palace with its "sheen of bronze, the blaze of gold and amber, silver, ivory too," a mansion he compares to "the boundless glory" of Zeus's court on Mount Olympus. The Phaeacians recognize Odysseus as a man of culture and good taste as he admires the beautiful art of the dancers of their country "who stamped the ground with marvelous pulsing steps as Odysseus gazed at their flying, flashing feet, his heart aglow with wonder." When he approaches the king's estate in Phaeacia and beholds the bountiful orchards and the ripe vineyards bearing pomegranates, pears, apples, figs, and olives, again Odysseus is awestruck at the luxuriance of nature's color and abundance, "gazing at all this bounty" and "marveling at it all". Thus homes which form sensitive hearts also cultivate an appreciation for the grace of beauty in all its various expressions whether it is the refinement of manners, the adornment of clothing, the beauty of the bard's poetry, or the miracle of the human body that recalls the beauty of a Greek god—Penelope resembling golden Aphrodite and Nausicaa inspiring Odysseus to marvel, "Princess, are you a goddess or a mortal? If one of the gods . . . you're Artemis to the life, the daughter of mighty Zeus."

All these virtues of the human heart—the hospitable heart that welcomes travelers, the kind heart that pities the miseries of wanderers, the loyal heart that remains faithful to family members, the tender heart that extends loving care to the young and to the elderly, the pure heart that governs the body with modesty, the grateful heart that remembers its unrepayable debts to parents and benefactors, and the sensitive heart that appreciates the wonder of beauty— are nourished in the home and form the essence of civilized manners and morals. Without these virtues of the human heart, cultures degenerate to the level of the barbaric. In the *Odyssey* the savage Cyclops—who live in crude, dark caves, not beautiful homes—possess hardened, cruel hearts and cannibalize travelers rather than welcoming them with hospitality. They have no sense of compassion or mercy for the hunger and homelessness of shipwrecked wanderers, attacking them with violence and brutality. Living as isolated individuals in dark caves with no sense of a family life or an extended family, they lack any concept of loyalty to relatives or tenderness for the young or elderly. Gluttonous in their appetites and animalistic in their behavior, the Cyclops of course have no concept of shame or modesty. Unlike the civilized that honor the gods with sacrifices and obey the law of gods that teaches the sacredness of hospitality, the Cyclops never express thanksgiving, "never blink at Zeus and Zeus's shield of storm and thunder, or any other blessed god." Knowing only how to live in the sense of survival and ignorant of the ideals of the true, the good, and the beautiful, the barbarians do not cultivate the fine arts—"the feast, the lyre and dance"—that flourish in civilized societies.

A world without the nurture of the home to cultivate the virtues of the heart degenerates to the level of the coarse, the vulgar, and the brutal. As the home and family are deconstructed with abortion, contraception, divorce, cohabitation, same-sex marriage, population decline, and embryonic stem-cell research, the civilizing virtues of the human heart do not govern society's moral norms and legal decisions. While the ancient Greeks acknowledged the sacredness of the laws commanding hospitality and kindness to strangers, the modern world does not welcome children into the world as over 50 million aborted babies in America since *Roe v. Wade* verify . While Homer's pagan society honored parents with the filial loyalty of the family bond and with the obligation of reverence for the elderly, the modern world feels no special duties toward the aged or dying and condones euthanasia or withholding nutrition as Terry Schiavo's example illustrates. While both Penelope and Odysseus in their loyalty honored their marital vows as the foundation of a civilized society

("What good sense resided in your Penelope—how well Icarius's daughter remembered you, Odysseus, the man she married once!" Agamemnon reflects), nearly half of marriages in the age of no-fault divorce are dissolved. While the noble women in the *Odyssey* were governed by the ideals of purity and were scandalized by immodesty and promiscuity—Odysseus calling his unloyal maids "You sluts—the suitors' whores"—couples in the twenty-first century shamelessly regard cohabitation as an acceptable alternative to marriage. Without the home's educational influence to form the virtues of the heart, the appreciation for beauty withers. When banal popular melodies replace Gregorian chant as sacred music, when casual clothing becomes appropriate attire for formal occasions and holy events, when watching violent or prurient films replaces the enjoyment of the arts , and when body piercings and tattoos become stylish, the modern world loses its sense of the transcendent, divine nature of beauty which the ancient Greeks celebrated in their homes, clothing, art, and poetry.

The culture of the home raises the conduct of human life and measures it by the highest standards, not the lowest common denominator. It does not tolerate immorality in the name of diversity or non-judgmentalism. When Odysseus returns to Ithaca, he shows no mercy to the suitors who abused his home, debauched the maidens, and plotted to murder his son. Neither he nor Penelope compromises moral principles and civilized ideals to accommodate the slatternly habits of the Suitors and their mistresses. Without these moral norms instilled by the home, the virtues of the heart do not influence the culture of a society. Instead of refined human beings with the virtues of the heart setting the norm, hardhearted, insensitive functionaries destroy innocent human life, experiment upon aborted human fetuses, administer euthanasia, seduce youth with contraceptives, deconstruct marriage, and unleash the cruelty of war. This dehumanization and "abolition of man" destroy the meaning of a human heart and all its noble sentiments, refined feelings, and works of mercy.

Chapter 7. The Magic of Childhood Memories in Andersen's "The Snow Queen"

Of the many gifts parents and adults offer children on birthdays and at Christmas, none of them surpasses the joy of fond memories from a happy childhood. These recollections leave a deposit of lifelong remembrances that nourish the spirit and keep a person young at heart. While the chronological period of childhood vanishes like all the seven ages of man, the fond memory of childhood remains indelibly imprinted in the consciousness of all persons regardless of age. It is one of life's greatest treasures that parents bequeath to children. As Aloysha remarks to a group of schoolboys in Dostoyevsky's *The Brothers Karamazov*:

> Remember that nothing is nobler, stronger, more vital, or more useful in future life than some happy memory, especially one from your childhood. A lot is said about upbringing, but the very best upbringing, perhaps, is some lovely, holy memory preserved from one's childhood. If a man carries many such memories with him, they will keep him safe throughout his life.

Robert Louis Stevenson's poem "To Willie and Henrietta" from *A Child's Garden of Verses* captures one of those "holy, lovely" memories that adults preserve forever. In the poem adults happily recall their own innocent childhood as they watch their children play: "Now in the elders' seat/ We rest with quiet feet, / And from the window-bay/ We watch the children, our successors play." Although the childhood of these parents disappeared all too quickly, their reminiscence keeps alive the taste of life's goodness: "'Time was,' the golden head/ Irrevocably said; / But time which none can bind, / While flowing fast away, leaves love behind." Regardless of age a person never forgets the exquisite moments of childhood that embody the sheer fun of play and the purest of joys, experiences that evoke a sense of wonder and gratitude for the great adventure of life. In Wordsworth's famous words from the poem "My Heart Leaps Up" that describes the marvel of beholding the rainbow, "The Child is father of the Man." That is, the period of childhood, the most formative and impressionable of ages, cultivates the human sensibilities and sensitizes the heart to marvel at the beautiful and the miraculous symbolized by the splendor of the rainbow, an experience that uplifts the mind to contemplate divine mysteries. The happy times shared between children and friends or between children and family members instill a love of life, reveal the beauty of innocence, and give childhood its magical aura—what Wordsworth in another poem calls "intimations of immortality."

As Hans Andersen shows in "The Snow Queen," of the many wiles the Devil devises to rob children of their innocence and deprive them of a sense of the miraculous, the holy, and the transcendent, the annihilation of the happy memories of childhood especially serves the cause of evil. In the story the broken glass from the Devil's mirror, entering the eye and the heart, perverts the good by corrupting the child's vision of wonder and by hardening the heart to reject love. In the fairy tale a boy and a girl enjoy the happy, innocent, carefree childhood that Dostoyevsky, Stevenson, and Wordsworth identify with holiness, love, and wonder. Playing always in the lovely rose garden, holding each other's hands, gazing at picture books, and singing "In the valley grew roses wild, / And there we spoke with the Holy Child," Kay and Gerda revel in their endearing friendship: "What beautiful summer days they were; how lovely it was to be outside near the fresh rose-trees, the fresh rose-trees that seemed as if they would never stop blooming!" This magical realm of childhood's innocent play and natural wonder, however, abruptly ends when Kay discovers a splinter of glass in his eye and another piece in his heart—broken pieces from the Devil's mirror that shattered into countless fragments when his School of Demons flew toward Heaven "to make fun of Our Lord and His Angels"—an evil of the magnitude of opening Pandora's box that releases into the world earthly Problems, evil Passions, many Cares, numerous Sorrows, and countless Diseases that are legion, as plentiful as insects in Hawthorne's version of the story in "The Paradise of Children" from *A Wonder Book*. In "The Snow Queen" these "hundreds of millions, billions, and even more pieces" of glass scattered throughout the world dull the eye's vision and turn the heart into a lump of ice that signifies the corruption of childhood. Cynicism replaces wonder, and criticism and sarcasm replace kindness and gratitude. Instead of admiring the beauty of the roses, Kay's distorted eyesight regards the roses as "worm-eaten," "lop-sided," and "disgusting."

Instead of cherishing the sweetness of Gerda's adoring friendship, he runs away from her companionship. Instead of marveling at the picture book, he ridicules it as "only fit for babies," and instead of marveling at the beauty of the snowflake, he reduces it to analysis under the microscope. Instead of honoring the grandmother who loves him dearly and reads to him, he criticizes the stories and mocks the old woman by mimicking her. In short, Kay is soon transported into the land of the Snow Queen, the loveless realm of frozen hearts and hardened feelings where his happy childhood becomes a lost memory.

Heartbroken at the sudden disappearance of her beloved friend, Gerda begins her long quest to find Kay and recapture their happy childhood. Although Kay is far removed in the distant land of the Snow Queen, Gerda's purity of heart—always recalling the beautiful summer days in the rose garden—never wavers in finding Kay and recovering his lost childhood. Sensing that Kay has been stolen, Gerda begins her long journey in earnest, pleading with the river, "Is it true that you've taken my little playmate? I'll make you a present of my red shoes if you'll give him back to me!" Their separation and the end of their friendship mark the loss of childhood wickedly "stolen" from both of the children. Climbing aboard a boat and drifting on the river, Gerda arrives at a cottage where a cunning witch welcomes her with the design of capturing the child and stopping Gerda's quest for Kay. Losing sight of her goal and distracted by the witch's offers of pleasure—a dish of delicious cherries, play in a beautiful garden, and "a lovely bed with a red silk eiderdown stuffed with blue violets"—Gerda is lulled and seduced by the clever witch whose evil magic makes all the roses disappear from her garden: "The old woman was afraid that if Gerda saw the roses she would think of her own, and then remember little Kay and run off." Like the Devil who uses the glass splinters to erase Kay's happy memories of childhood, the witch manipulates her crooked stick to wilt all the roses. Both the Devil and the witch do harm by destroying the innocence of children. They resent the formidable power of a happy childhood as a potent force of goodness that undoes the multiplication of evil produced by the millions of glass splinters. They use their wiles to cast spells that erase memories and make the wonder of childhood vanish.

With no roses in the witch's garden to recall her happy days with Kay in their own flower garden, Gerda loses contact with her precious past and remains bound by the spell of the witch. But one day she accidentally happens to notice the rose on the old woman's hat:

> 'Why!' cried Gerda. 'Aren't there any roses here?' And she ran among the flower-beds, searching and searching. Her hot tears fell just where a rose-tree had sunk into the earth, and as her warm tears moistened the ground, the tree shot up at once, just as full of bloom as when it disappeared; and throwing her arms around it, Gerda kissed the roses and thought about the lovely roses at home—and with them, about little Kay.

The sudden chain of association of seeing a rose on the hat to being moved to tears to shedding tears on the ground to seeing the roses bloom to remembering the rose garden at home to recalling Kay restores Gerda's temporarily lost childhood and calls to mind the glorious days of summer she briefly forgot. As Andersen shows, these golden memories never disappear. They recede into the background, they are forgotten for a short time, or other thoughts preoccupy the mind and prevent it from remembering the magical sweetness of life that a true childhood retains, but the happy memories never die. One can no more forget one's childhood than deny one's mother and father. As Gerda's reactions demonstrate, the past memories of a joyful childhood combat the wiles of evil and find release from the power of malevolence. To cite again Alyosha's words from *The Brothers Karamazov*, "If a man carries many such memories with him, they will keep him safe throughout his life." They lead a person back to the true sources of happiness and to the joys of simple pleasures and away from the temptations of the world, the flesh, and the devil. No matter how far a person wanders like Kay into the remote land of ice and no matter how long a person delays from the right course like Gerda in the realm of the witch, the memory of childhood provides a way back to life's deepest origins of goodness.

Escaping from the magic of the witch by recovering her childhood, Gerda continues her search for Kay. Everywhere she travels her childlike charm and innocent sweetness—the fruits of delightful play in the rose garden—melt the hearts of all whom she encounters. Everyone befriends her, extends special help to ease her journey, and feels touched by the little girl's purity of heart and ingenuous question: "Tell me, if you can, where I shall find my playfellow?" A prince offers Gerda hospitality, clothes her with silk and velvet, provides a muff and boots, and presents her with "a new carriage of pure gold" when he bids her farewell, "the heaviest leave-taking of all." In her next encounter Gerda's travels lead her from a prince's palace to a robbers' castle where an old hag polishes her knife to devour the little girl as "a little fatted lamb" and where Gerda is forced to sleep with the violent robber girl who goes to bed with a knife in one hand. Yet Gerda's angelic presence and gentle sweetness have the same magical effect on the robber girl that they produced on the prince. Even this hardened little girl is moved by Gerda's heartwarming story and promises, "I'll see what I can do for you!" as she commands her reindeer, "I'm going to undo your rope and help you to get away so that you can run off to Lapland, but you must put your best foot forward and take this little girl to the Snow Queen's palace where her playmate is." Like the Prince, the robber girl too cannot do enough for Gerda as she provides her with two loaves and a ham and warns the reindeer "but see you take good care of the little girl." Thus the simple, guileless Gerda resists the witch, enchants the prince, and touches the heart of the hardened robber girl. Her irresistible charm comes from an innocent childhood nourished by the memories of play in the rose garden with Kay. As long as Gerda retains the fond reminiscences of her past and does not lose sight of her dear friend, she exerts a mysterious influence of goodness upon all who meet her. Wherever she tells her poignant story of loss and sadness "with such beseeching tearful eyes", she evokes the kindness of strangers who offer gifts, help, and special favors. When the reindeer implores the Finnish woman to give Gerda supernatural powers to overcome the redoubtable Snow Queen, the old woman remarks, "I can't give her greater powers than she has already.

Can't you see how great that is? Can't you see how she makes man and beast serve her, and how well she's made her way in the world on her own bare feet? She mustn't know of her power from us—it comes from her heart, it comes of her being a sweet innocent child." The secret of Gerda's mysterious power, then, originates in her pure heart educated in her childhood. A beautiful, sunny rose garden of innocent play and an atmosphere of love form her heart and fill it with a treasury of memories. The precious memories bestow upon a child a power or "charm" that warms human hearts and melts Snow Queens who cannot withstand a child's unspoiled goodness. These heartwarming memories strengthen and inspire Gerda throughout her long, arduous journey to the land of the Snow Queen and repel the evil influences of witches and robbers. A little girl unconscious of her "power" conquers devils, witches, hags, robber girls, and snow queens.

Once Gerda discovers the land of ice and snow where Kay is a prisoner in the Snow Queen's palace, she sees a vast gloomy space of one hundred halls devoid of every form of play and every trace of childhood: "Gaiety never came this way," neither a dance for the bears, card-playing, or fun during a coffee hour, Andersen writes. Instead of playing in a rose garden, looking at picture books, singing songs, or holding hands with Gerda, "Kay sat quite alone in the vast empty hall of ice, many miles in length, and gazed at the pieces of ice, thinking and thinking until his head creaked with the effort." Even after Gerda greets Kay with affectionate hugs and calls him by name ("Kay! Dear little Kay! I've found you after all!"), he shows no recollection or emotion, hardened in heart and frozen in feeling. Surprised by great joy, Gerda begins to weep warm tears that fall upon Kay's breast and soon enter his heart, melting the lump of ice and releasing the splinter of glass. Once Gerda sings the words of the familiar hymn from their childhood days ("In the valley grew roses wild, /And there we spoke with the Holy Child!"), Kay suddenly remembers, and the Snow Queen's spell instantly breaks. Kay's memories of childhood flood his soul and melt his hardness: "Then Kay burst into tears; he wept so desperately that the grain of glass was washed out of his eye; he recognized her and cried joyfully, 'Gerda! Dear little Gerda!' "

This, then, is the power of the sweet innocent the Finnish woman recognized. The memory of this song brings the children back to their beginnings and rekindles all the heartfelt memories they formed in the bond of love. Once Gerda kisses Kay's cheeks, eyes, hands and feet, the warmth of love melts all the hardness and coldness that the Snow Queen inflicted upon the boy. Gerda and Kay now retrace their steps homeward and reminisce about grandmother and the roses in the garden. They travel hand in hand to the site of their fondest memories, returning to the familiar places of the past: the high towers, the big city, grandmother's door, the living room, and the little stools: "Kay and Gerda sat down in their own seats and held each other's hands. Grandmother was sitting there in God's bright sunshine and reading aloud from the Bible, 'Except ye become as little children, ye shall not enter into the kingdom of heaven.'" Again it is summer, but the children have grown up and left their childhood, "yet children still, children at heart." This backward movement from the faraway palace of the Snow Queen to the familiar surrounding of the rose garden is the road of memory that leads to the magic of childhood, a road that recovers what William Blake called the "songs of innocence." This road of memory preserves a person's goodness by returning him to the love of a grandmother, the beauty of a garden, the goodness of laughter, and the closeness of God.

As Andersen's story illustrates, these happy childhood memories keep a person in love with life and keep adults of all ages "children at heart". They protect a person from becoming lost in the world in the way Kay wandered into the vast halls of the Snow Queen's palace. They rescue a person from the cynicism and jadedness of a world ruled by doubt rather than by wonder. They bring a person back again to the eternal springs of joy and prevent the heart of love from freezing into a lump of ice. They safeguard a person from the snares and wickedness of the Devil and the witches seeking to entice the innocent with temptation. They remind a person of the beauty of simplicity and the goodness of natural things like roses, gardens, play, friendship, and families. They nourish an appreciation for close, affectionate relationships of love and friendship that create these unforgettable moments of a lifetime. Without Kay's grandmother's love, without Gerda's affection for her friend, without the children holding hands, and without mothers and fathers and brothers and sisters enjoying their time together playing and tasting the sweetness of life, the child would never be the father of the man, "holy, lovely memories" would never accompany a person in his life's journey, and the march of time would never "leave love behind."

Chapter 8. Crucified Love and Martyrdom in Shakespeare's *King Lear*

Christ's unspeakable agony in His passion and death illustrates the crucified nature of love which embraces suffering and sacrifice. The gift of love, of course, obligates a person to return love for love, to feel indebted always for an unrepayable gift. Because God loved man first, man is bound to love God with all his mind and heart as the First Commandment teaches. Because parents love their children first with tenderness and generosity, children owe honor to their father and mother and feel the duty to care for them in their old age as small repayment for all the parental love they received in a lifetime. One reason a woman falls in love with a man and marries him is that he loved her first as many famous love stories like *Romeo and Juliet* and *Pride and Prejudice* illustrate. In responding "yes" to a man's proposal of marriage, a woman offers the gift of herself in self-donation as gratitude for a man's appreciation for the blessing of a beautiful woman and his promise of marriage and fidelity. Love deserves love. To be loved obliges a person to love in return and to give as one receives. "If you love me, you will keep my commandments," Christ said, indicating the reciprocal nature of love and love's debt to the donor.

However, in the fallen world of original sin, divine and human love often go unrewarded or spurned. In the parable of the ten lepers when Christ miraculously cured all ten, only one returned to give thanks: "Were not all ten healed?" Christ asks in disappointment of those who receive love but do not return it. The Israelites, whom God favored with His Divine Providence, special revelation, and miracles of the Red Sea and the manna in the wilderness, turned to false gods, murmured in the wilderness, and rejected the Messiah in their hardheartedness. Many ungrateful children exploit their parents for their money, ignore them in their old age, and do not please or honor them in gratitude for the gift of life. In many marriages ruined by divorce, the gift of self goes unrequited as husband or wife exploits the other for money or pleasure or fails to love, cherish, and honor the other until death. In other words, love often suffers crucifixion and a broken heart despite all its generosity and sacrifices. To love as Christ loves is always to be vulnerable—to give and not to receive, to love and not be loved, to bless and never to hear a word of gratitude. As Christ explained in one of his hard sayings to his disciples, "If they hated me, they will hate you"—a warning about the crucified nature of Christian love that is always subject to rejection and persecution.

Even though this vulnerable, crucified love appears unrequited or fruitless, it is never wasted or useless even though it goes unappreciated. Christ's ostensibly futile suffering and ignominious death saved man from damnation and gained him eternal life. In Augustine's *Confessions*, his mother Monica's pure, unconditional love for her son's soul appeared wasted as Augustine scorned his mother's teaching about chastity and mocked her practice of the Christian faith to follow the pagan customs of Rome or adopt the Manichaean heresy.

However, her suffering was not in vain, for a bishop advised the heartbroken Monica that her tears and sorrows that pleaded for her decadent son's conversion would touch the heart of God: "It is impossible that a child of such tears should perish." After Augustine rejected the various pagan heresies that darkened his mind and debauched his life, he attributed his change from the darkness of error to the truth of the Gospel to his mother's crucified love. Christ-like love, then, does not count the cost, gives until it hurts, returns good for evil, and is unafraid of suffering and sacrifice. As Christ's agony on the Cross illustrates, crucified love is fruitful and miraculous. Christ's infinite love that assented to crucifixion and the blood of martyrs suffering death for their faith prove that this great love is fecund because it produces seed, fruit, and resurrection. As Mother Francis writes in *Anima Christi*, "We shall give life to no one except at the cost of some dying of ours." She continues, "If we do not wish to die, we cannot delude ourselves into thinking that we can be purveyors of life."

Of all Shakespeare's plays *King Lear* especially illuminates the nature of crucified love and the price of martyrdom. Even though the action of this tragedy occurs in pre-Christian England, Cordelia, the heroine who suffers merciless persecution both from Lear and from the tyrant Edmund, epitomizes Christ-like love by risking her life for her father and forgiving him for his sin. Her example illuminates the entire book of Christian love: purity of heart, a life of service, forgiveness of those who have trespassed against her, and self-sacrifice. In Elizabethan England where Catholics were fined, imprisoned, hanged, or martyred as the examples of Saint Thomas More, Saint John Fisher, Edmund Campion, and

Robert Southwell recall, a dramatist's incorporation of the Catholic faith required indirection and subtlety—a code language as Joseph Pearce explains in *The Quest for Shakespeare*, a book that makes a compelling argument for Shakespeare's Catholicism. Despite the pagan setting of *King Lear* in pre-Christian England, the play deals with the subject of martyrdom, a theme no doubt influenced by the heroic deaths of the devout Catholics who suffered for their faith rather than conform to the Anglican Church and accept the Oath of Supremacy. In Act I when Lear is dividing his inheritance and retiring from his kingship, he asks his three daughters to proclaim their love before he grants them their portion of his estate. Goneril flatters her aged father with pompous exaggeration: "Sir, I love you more than word can wield the matter; / Dearer than eyesight, space, and liberty, / Beyond what can be loved, rich or rare, / No less than life, with grace, health, beauty, honor." The second daughter also boasts of her boundless love for her father, adding "I find she names my very deed of love; / Only she comes too short. . . ." In other words, both daughters acquiesce to a required oath to remain in the official favor of a ruling power. When Cordelia, the youngest daughter, declares her love for Lear, she avoids the fulsome adulation of her sisters, speaking simply and sincerely that she honors her father as a grateful, dutiful daughter: "You have begot me, bred me, lov'd me. I / Return those duties back as are right fit, / Obey you, love, and most honor you." When Cordelia protests that her sisters' profession of love approaches bombast—"Why have my sisters husbands if they say they love you all?"—Lear in a rage disowns his daughter, deprives her of her inheritance, and swears to estrange himself from her forever. That is, Cordelia suffers grave consequences for her nonconformity to the dictates of political authority. Cordelia's true love for her father deserves a father's gratitude, not his hateful wrath. Lear's vehement temper and cruel words inflict an unjust punishment upon an innocent child as Cordelia becomes a victim of crucified love—a martyr. For speaking the truth with integrity and for honoring her father with filial love, Cordelia receives hate for love. Cordelia gives but does not receive. She renders justice but suffers injustice. Thus her love for her father appears wasted because it goes unappreciated and unrewarded. In short, Cordelia's refusal to obey the threats of her prideful father for whom might is right resembles a loyal Catholic's fearless defiance of conformity to the Church of England.

However, King Lear also suffers the fate of crucified love. After Lear divides his wealth between his flattering daughters, Goneril and Regan betray their father as they announce their extravagant oaths of love only in order to gain his fortune. Soon abandoned by his two ungrateful daughters who treat the aged king as a lowly servant and who treat their venerable father as a petulant child, Lear finds himself a homeless beggar in the cataclysm of a vehement storm because he rejected the unjust conditions stipulated by his daughters. They offer him shelter in their castles at the price of divesting himself of his one hundred retainers—the symbol of kingship. Like Catholics who suffer grave consequences for not assenting to the Oath of Supremacy, Lear either conforms to his daughters' terms or suffers cruel punishment, exposure to the violent forces of the tempest that remind Lear of his daughters' betrayal: "Rumble thy bellyful! Spit, fire! Spit, rain! / Nor rain, wind, thunder, fire, are my daughters. / I tax you not, you elements, with unkindness; / I never gave you kingdom, call'd you children, / You owe me no subscription." Lear himself now experiences the pain of martyrdom, a crucified love, crying out, "Ingratitude, thou marble-hearted fiend, / More hideous when thou show'st thee in a child/ Than the sea-monster" and "How sharper than a serpent's tooth it is/ To have a thankless child." Lear expostulates, "I gave you all." Like Cordelia's goodness, Lear's generosity to his daughters receives nothing in return. He gives his entire wealth to Goneril and Regan but receives only contempt and rejection—not even shelter in their castle during a ferocious storm when, as Cordelia says, "Mine enemy's dog,/ Though he had bit me, should have stood that night/ Against my fire." Cordelia and Lear, then, share a common fate as their gifts of love are despised rather than valued, Cordelia banished as a worthless daughter with no dowry and Lear disowned by his scheming daughters as a cantankerous old man. Cordelia objects to the "oath" of love demanded by her father in his display of power, and Lear refuses to compromise the truth of his natural authority as both king and father and to "conform" to unjust laws—father and daughter revealing the courage of martyrs inspired by a passion for truth and love of justice.

Because Lear's munificent generosity and Cordelia's pure heart go unacknowledged and do not receive their due, the moral crisis of the play calls into question the entire purpose of marriage, family, and love. To give all and receive nothing, to sow and never to reap, to work and receive no reward, to do good and suffer evil makes no sense and questions the validity of the moral law. During Lear's cruel suffering and temporary madness on the heath during the tempest, human life appears devoid of meaning because the gift of love ostensibly bears fruit. When Lear invokes Mother Nature to curse the human race and annihilate the reproduction of the species ("Strike flat the thick rotundity o' the world! Crack nature's molds, all germains [seeds] spill at once/ That makes ingrateful man!"), he decries the futility of love. The love, care, and riches Lear has expended in a whole lifetime of devotion to his daughters has produced unloving, selfish daughters who resemble "pelicans" and "tigers" as he calls Goneril and Regan. In the light of Lear's great suffering, the offspring of marital human love appear no different from bastards conceived in animal lust. To Lear the moral distinctions between "legitimate" children born in marriage and "illegitimate" children conceived out of wedlock count for nothing, for he argues, "Let copulation thrive; for Gloucester's bastard son/ Was kinder to his father than my daughters/ Got 'tween the lawful sheets." Irate with righteous indignation at life's callous injustice in which goodness is punished with evil, Lear sees the world as a vicious animal kingdom that breaks man's heart and torments man's mind with a sense of nihilism, "a tale told by an idiot, full of sound and fury signifying nothing" to cite Shakespeare's words in *Macbeth*. Crucified love exacts a great price for following one's conscience and following the law of love. To suffer as a Catholic in Elizabethan England is the equivalent of King Lear's exposure to the terror of the storm. The fire, thunder, wind, and rain that attack Lear resemble the fines, ostracism, imprisonment, torture, or death that assailed the English martyrs.

However, the brokenhearted and disillusioned king escapes dark fatalism or cynical despair because Cordelia brings succor to her father in his most abject misery. She redeems the world for him, restoring the meaning of love and proving that human beings possess hearts of love, not stone. Leaving the comfort of her marriage to the Duke of Burgundy in France and risking her life, she returns to England in the midst of civil war to relieve her father's suffering. Love returns love. Love does not give in order to receive but gives with no thought of gain. Love gives all and does not count the cost. Crucified love is willing even to die for the beloved, and Cordelia pays the price of her life in her gift of love to her aging and dying father as she is imprisoned and executed. Although inflicted with injustice by her father's wrath, Cordelia continues to do justice without hatred or vengeance. Cordelia treats her father with the gentleness of a daughter's grateful love, never forgetting her filial debt to her parent as she says ". . . let this kiss/ Repair those violent harms that my two sisters/ Have in thy reverence made." An innocent child forgives her father's tragic flaw and loves him despite his sin. Crucified love never returns evil for evil and never identifies justice with revenge. When Lear and Cordelia are reunited and reconciled, he feels rescued from death to life: "You do me wrong to take me out o' th' grave." Cordelia's fidelity to her father changes his whole life from a sense of despair and futility to a feeling of fruitfulness and meaning. Her crucified love that returns good for evil restores Lear's dignity, sanity, and peace even in a destructive world where the tempestuous passions of avarice, wrath, and lust rage. The offering of crucified love acts as a potent seed with unimaginable fecundity and potent curative power.

Crucified love—the courage and patience of enduring suffering out of love for the truth, of sacrificing worldly prosperity for the sake of a moral principle, and of heroically dying for the sake of justice as both Lear and Cordelia do—epitomizes the essence of martyrdom. In a tragic world filled with great chaos—the devastation of the storm, the anarchy of a civil war between jealous sisters, the unspeakable sufferings of an aged man struggling to preserve his life and sanity, and the cruelty inflicted upon a saintly woman of pure heart—the heroism of crucified love is life-giving, purgative, and curative in both spiritual and physical ways. For example, crucified love proves that man's life is not as "cheap as beast's" because it restores dignity and honor to human nature. In their martyrdom both Cordelia and Lear act according to the highest moral ideals and refuse to debase themselves to fawn for favor. Instead of capitulating to Goneril and Regan's arrogant command to divest himself of all the symbols of kingship in order to be a guest in their castles—the very castles the king bequeathed to them in his retirement—Lear demands his due as a father and king deserving of respect and filial piety. Refusing to welcome their father as a venerable king entitled to his retinue, Goneril and Regan object to the number of retainers that attend him, protesting "What, fifty followers?" and then complaining "What need you five and twenty, ten, or five. . . .?" and then arguing "What need one?" Lear's impassioned answer to these objections inspires the fire of courage and invigorates the heart of a martyr for whom moral truth flashes with new vigor:

> O, reason not the need! Our basest beggars
> are in the poorest thing superfluous.

Allow not nature more than nature needs,

Man's life 's cheap as beast's. Thou art a lady;

If only to go warm were gorgeous,

Why, nature needs not what thou gorgeous wear'st,

Which scarcely keeps thee warm. (II.iv.67-73)

Man is more than an animal with an outer covering to protect him from the elements. Just as human beings beautify themselves with articles of clothing that mirror their dignity rather than merely protect themselves from cold, they also live for other reasons beyond survival. If a woman's finery or a king's attendants are removed as unnecessary or useless, then man is debased to the primitive level of subsistence and becomes "a thin, bare, forked animal" with rags rather than a woman resplendent in her beauty or a king majestic in his glory. In Lear's agony of crucified love he fearlessly revives a great moral truth that the world renounces. Refusing to stoop to base dehumanization by surviving at the cost of honor and integrity, Lear's moral conviction gives tongues of flame to the truth, and he carries the cross that loving, defending, and suffering for the truth require. Lear cries out, "You heavens, give me that patience, patience I need!" The purity of crucified love cures a corrupt world of its ugly sinfulness. Cordelia's sacrificial love salves the pain raging in Lear's heart and mind from the attack of the storm and from the wound of ingratitude. In the darkest night of his soul, Lear hears the heartwarming, life-giving words of his beloved daughter: "O my dear father! Restoration hang/ Thy medicine on my lips, and let this kiss/ Repair those violent harms that my two sisters/ Have in thy reverence made." The witness of crucified love, then, redeems a sinful world. Cordelia's thankful heart more than compensates for the ingratitude of her sisters, and Lear's noble courage and contrite heart more than compensate for his tragic flaw that banished his beloved daughter.

Even though *King Lear* ends tragically with the deaths of Lear and Cordelia, their crucified loves have profound consequences. Cordelia redeems the world for Lear because his love for his children has produced the charitable heart of a saintly daughter and not been spent in vain. She redeems the world for her father because she treats him with the reverence, kindness, and thankfulness that rescue human life from barbarism. Lear redeems the world for all who witness his heroic moral courage, inspiring them by his passion for justice, honor, and dignity and suffering humiliation and persecution for his love of truth. His loyal servant Kent marvels, "The wonder is he hath endured so long." He impresses upon everyone's memory a heroic image of man as "The beauty of the world, the paragon of animals" to quote from *Hamlet*. Only because crucified love is willing to die to self and to die for another does the world change for the better. Only when noble men and women "give all" as Lear and Cordelia do without computing self-interest or worrying about the worldly consequences does the world remain human, civilized, and exalted.

Although Shakespeare in Protestant Elizabethan England does not allude in *King Lear* to martyrdom for the faith, Cordelia and Lear suffer as innocent persecuted victims who die—like Christ and the English martyrs—for the sake of the truth and as the result of the sins of others. They both carry their crosses and empty themselves, sparing no personal act of love in their self-sacrifice. Their deaths appear wasted, for as Lear pleads with Cordelia dead in his arms, "Why should a dog, a horse, a rat, have life, / And thou no breath at all?" However, Lear's and Cordelia's resistance to evil ends the reign of tyranny in England, restores rightful rule, and reestablishes the primacy of the family as the center of the civilization of love. Without Cordelia's constant love for her father and without Lear's unwavering passion for justice, the tempest on the heath, the madness of avarice, and the anarchy of civil war would annihilate every vestige of humanity, civilization, and morality like the devastating winds that Lear invokes to crush a world in violation of the natural law that bonds fathers and daughters:

> Blow, winds, and crack your cheeks! Rage! blow!
>
> You cataracts and hurricanes, spout
>
> Till you have drench'd our steeples, drown'd the cocks! (III.ii.1-3)

In Shakespeare's play this violent storm—the sum of all the wanton forces of injustice that unleash untold suffering upon innocent victims—epitomizes the fallen world of war and the sinful nature of man in need of redemption. This redemption comes through the heroic deaths of two "martyrs"—Cordelia the martyr of love and Lear the martyr of truth who both refuse—like the

English martyrs of Shakespeare's day—to be sycophants in order to inherit a fortune, to preserve life, or to gain the world at the cost of their soul. Crucified love, then, not only restores civilization, comforts the broken heart, and purifies evil but also transcends fear and exalts human nature. This is the fruitfulness of sacrificial love that is always life-bearing, curative, purgative, and never spent in vain.

Chapter 9. The Treasure or Prizes of Life

"For where your treasure is, there will your heart be also." Christ's words acknowledge the simple truth that all human beings cherish their possessions and gifts. However, many value things of secondary importance or overestimate worldly goods, failing to distinguish between the pearls of great price from gold, silver, and expensive luxuries. While all persons seek prizes, rewards, and benefits from their labors, real treasure transcends the financial value of money and material riches. While Christ's teaching refers to the treasure of eternal life, the fruitfulness of love, and the joys of the Beatitudes as the great rewards of loving God and loving neighbor, Homer's ancient wisdom also illuminates the distinction between real treasure and worldly gain.

Throughout the *Iliad* Homer illuminates the truth that human life acquires purpose and meaning from the prizes or rewards a person earns from war, athletic contests, and work. At the beginning of the epic Achilles resents the arrogance of Agamemnon robbing him of his prize Briseis, the woman whom Achilles considers a trophy of war for his heroic deeds on behalf of the Greeks in the Trojan War: "And now you threaten to strip me of my prize in person—the one I fought for long and hard, and sons of Achaea handed her to me." Agamemnon demands Achilles' prize because the god Apollo requires him to return his earlier prize, Chryseis, the daughter of the god's priest Chryses: "But fetch me another prize," Agamemnon demands, "and straight off too, else I alone of the Argives go without my honor." The great heroes of Greece and Troy—Patroclus, Hector, Achilles—also receive the prizes of honor and glory for their valorous deeds on the battlefield—honor and glory that the solemn funeral rites of Patroclus and Hector afford these heroes through the gift of immortality. In the many battles throughout the epic, the heroic victors seize other prizes like the armor, shield, or horses of their defeated foes as their trophies.

Homer, however, depicts another form of prize during the funeral games on behalf of Patroclus. During these athletic competitions in chariot racing, boxing, wrestling, and the footrace, Achilles awards the winners prizes like mixing bowls, a battle-shield and helmet, a mare, a cauldron, a woman, and an ox. All the competitors, regardless of placing first or last, earn prizes, and even the elderly Nestor, past his prime for competition, receives a jar with double handles as trophy for his earlier accomplishments: "You never forget my friendship, never miss a chance to pay me the honor I deserve." Both in the fierce struggles of war and in the athletic contests the prize signifies the importance of rewards as forms of justice, tokens of accomplishments, and expressions of life's noblest aims. To fight and never gain a prize or to compete and never to receive a trophy lends futility to human effort and deprives work of a sense of achievement or productivity. Without these rewards human life resembles the punishment of Sisyphus in the underworld, the mindless monotony of pushing the rock up a hill only to see it roll to the bottom and repeat the process again and again—work which symbolizes futility. Prizes, gifts, and rewards give special meaning and purpose to a human being's life.

On the shield of Achilles many designs portray the importance of the prize as the mark of civilized life. In the city at peace the elders judge a case at law and deliberate to render a verdict, "a prize for the judge who'd speak the straightest verdict." In a scene of tilling and sowing, plowmen cultivate the ground and earn their just reward: "as they'd reach the end-strip, moving into the turn, a man would run up quickly and hand them a cup of honeyed, mellow wine. . . ." In a harvest scene where laborers cut, bind, and carry the grain during the busyness of the morning's work, the reward for their labor awaits them as servants prepare the slaughtered ox "while attendant women poured out barley, generous, glistening handfuls strewn for the reapers' midday meal." All these images depict the reward of honest labor that cooperates with nature's laws and rhythms—using the mind to reach a wise decision, sowing the seed at spring to reap the harvest in the fall, performing the day's labor to enjoy the leisure of rest. Without the incentive of the prize of just reward or grateful acknowledgment, life either acquires the brutishness of war—seizing and plundering the armor, women, or wealth of other nations—or resembles the futility of Hades where the dead spirits never taste the joy of winning or know the fulfillment of completing honorable labor that contributes to life's highest purposes.

Homer, then, distinguishes between the prizes of war, the rewards of civilization, and the useless wandering of the underworld. Although great warriors win glory and immortality for their heroic deeds and acquire the armor, horses, women, and gold of their enemies, they gain these prizes in the business of devastation and at the expense of destroying another city. The trophy of immortal fame often corresponds to the hero's short, glorious life which ends prematurely like a young sapling cut down before maturity. In the *Odyssey* the ghost of Achilles in Hades laments that he would rather live as a serf on earth performing the most menial work than be king of the dead. In other words, all the glories of war and all the tributes of fame do not compensate for dying young and leaving incomplete the work of a father, husband, and son in caring for a family and repaying parents in their old age for their loving care. In short, the spoils of war that dazzle with their brightness do not ultimately amount to true treasure.

The great prizes of civilization do not have the material worth of riches or the glory of immortal fame at the cost of early death. However, they possess an undying, enduring quality of their own as they provide the joy of knowing that one has preserved a noble heritage, one has lived in tune with nature's great purposes, and one has contributed to the abundance of life's harvest. For this reason Homer praises the great achievement of Penelope, the faithful wife who defended her home, upheld her marital vows, and formed the heart and conscience of her son during Odysseus's absence: "The fame of her virtue will never die. The immortal gods will lift a song for all mankind, a glorious song in praise of self-possessed Penelope." The great reward of civilization is fruitfulness, the knowledge that a family's faithful love has borne fruition in the happiness of another generation, in the joy of both giving and receiving loving care, in the completeness of sowing and reaping, and in the satisfaction of working and gaining the fruits of one's labor. This prize of civilization Homer illuminates in the final scene of the *Odyssey* when Odysseus reveals his identity to his father by a fond memory from childhood when father and son planted trees: "I begged you for everything I saw, a little boy trailing you through the orchard, picking our way among those trees, and you named them one by one. You gave me thirteen pear, ten apple trees, and forty figs. . . ." Thus Odysseus' homecoming, the embrace of husband and wife, and the reunion of father and son embody the greatest of prizes, more precious than any plunder from war or glory from battle, because family members behold the fruitfulness of love and perpetuate the noble legacy they inherited.

However, the prizes of modern life do not resemble the rewards of civilized life in Homer's epics or Christ's meaning of "treasure" in the highest sense. While the modern world awards handsome prizes to World Series victors, Super Bowl champions, and Academy Awards winners, these rewards offer only fame and wealth. Political victories in elections confer the trophies of prestige and power but do not guarantee the preservation of the moral norms of life. Victory in the modern world means success in war, politics, business, and athletics, but the fruits of civilized family life never receive the kudos that Homer affords them in his portraits of war and peace in the *Iliad* and *Odyssey*. With some exceptions like Robert Frost's "The Death of the Hired Man" (Home is "Something you somehow haven't to deserve"), few modern works of literature praise the greatness of fatherhood and motherhood, admire the glory of the family, or value the fruits of civilized order as Homer does. Just as Agamemnon and Achilles feud about the prize of Briseis and victorious soldiers strip off the armor

119

of their foes as valuable trophies, the modern mind also overestimates the possessions of material things and the profits from war and fails to appreciate the more precious rewards of civilization—the stability of a rhythmic life lived in tune with the laws of nature and the natural law that produce the fruitfulness of families. What is the gain of a pre-emptive war in Iraq—the discovery of weapons, the control of oil, the spread of democracy in the Middle East—compared to the loss of lives, the annihilation of marriages, and the suffering of widows and orphans? Like the Trojan War that unleashed the atrocities of war which destroyed families, the Iraq War also has devastated civilized life by the violent toll that war inflicts on nations. As Hector's wife Andromache laments at the end of the *Iliad*, "Now you go down to the House of death. . . and leave me here to waste away, a widow lost in the royal halls—and the boy only a baby, you and I so doomed."

Like Agamemnon's arrogant license which seized Achilles' prize for the sake of his own pleasure or "honor," the modern liberal mind makes an absolute value of freedom and exaggerates the meaning of "rights" to demand the euthanasia of the elderly, the abortion of babies, and same-sex marriages. These so-called prizes or political victories also involve the same wanton rape and plunder that the barbarism of war unleashes in its slaughter of sons and husbands. Because the horror of war destroys all the bonds of family life that create civilization, Priam and Hecuba lament the heart-breaking loss of their beloved son Hector that stirs the depths of their souls, Priam crying "stabbing grief for him will take me down to Death" and Hecuba grieving "O my child—my desolation! How can I go on living? What agonies must I suffer now, now *you* are dead and gone." The modern culture of death and divorce is as violent and brutal in its destruction of the family as The Trojan War in its effects of destroying civilization. Upon hearing of the death of her husband Hector, a sword pierces the heart of Andromache: "The world went black as night before her eyes, she fainted, falling backward, gasping away her life breath." Homer realistically portrays war as a form of barbarism that rends asunder all the deepest bonds of human hearts. Andromache grieves for her infant son with inconsolable sorrow: "Hector, what help are you to him, now you are dead?" The prize of war, then, offers only Pyrrhic victory for the conqueror and cruel injustice for the innocent victims.

Like the treasure of a wealthy city that tempts the avarice of the victors of war, the prize of money that rules oil companies, creates the usury of credit card companies, and dominates global trade also worships trophies gained at the expense of others. The modern world eyes prizes in the same light that Agamemnon views the just deserts of others—as his rightful possessions to be seized by raw force in an exercise of "might makes right". On the shield of Achilles Homer juxtaposes two cities, a city at peace where wedding feasts, songs, and dancing celebrate the prize of love that founds families and creates civilization and a city at war where an army attacks a nation "to plunder the city" or hoard "the handsome citadel stored within its depths." Wherever money rather than love is the pearl of great price, a people do not live in harmony or cooperation but suffer what Homer calls "Strife and Panic." As big government spends trillions of dollars in war and billions of dollars in bailouts and always increases taxes, a beleaguered people view themselves as exploited victims of a powerful government uncontrollable in its avarice and wastefulness. As American foreign policy fantasizes about benevolent American empires in the Middle East and imagines wars in Iraq and in Iran as trophies of oil, the treasure once again becomes the wanton seizing of another's rightful possessions rather than the growing and harvesting of fruit on one's own soil with the toil of one's own hands. In another scene on the shield Homer depicts "a thriving vineyard loaded with clusters, bunches of lustrous grapes in gold, ripening deep purple"—a harvest scene where boys and girls pick the fruit, "their hearts leaping in innocence, bearing away the sweet ripe fruit in wicker baskets." This picture on the shield illustrates the essence of civilization, harvesters gleaning the fruits of their own labor, producing a bountiful harvest, and rejoicing in nature's fertility. The greatest prizes are awarded when man's arts cooperate with nature's laws and God's Providence to produce abundance—not when war or business plunders the land or possessions of others.

Because modern man desires the spoils or war or usury gained from others, values treasures measured by money, and seeks the ephemeral worldly fame of victories, it depreciates the wealth created by one's own hands, by acts of love, or by creative powers. All of the scenes on the shield of Achilles that capture the essence of civilization as the art of living well depict humble persons performing the ordinary business of life with consummate skill or masterful art as they rejoice in nature's copious bounty. Using the natural powers of their own mind, hands, or body, they marvel at what they have produced with Mother Nature's cooperation. As the brides proceed to their wedding feasts, "women rushed to the doors and each stood moved with wonder" to behold the harvest of the family's love and the beginnings of a new generation. As the elders deliberate a case at law, the prize of bars of gold awards the gift to the judge whose native intelligence offers the wisest verdict. As the plowmen till the fields using their manual skills, they delight in the accomplishments of their physical labor as "the earth churned black beside them, like earth churning, solid gold it was." As the harvesters on the king's estate reap, bind, and carry the grain, the king rejoices in the happiness of governing a peaceful people who work for the common good and contribute to the needs of their society: "And there in the midst the king . . . stood tall in silence, rejoicing in his heart." As the youthful pickers gather the grapes in the vineyards "bearing away the sweet ripe fruit in wicker baskets," they too taste the sweetness of life's abundance as they accompany their work with music, "frisking, singing, shouting, their dancing steps beating out the time." In all of these pictures of civilized life, people enjoy the simple prizes they earn from the practice of their honest work or the use of their natural talent. Mothers raising their daughters, intelligent men using their minds, farmers performing their labor of love, kings governing out of a care for their people, and young men and women dancing and singing in their love of life all receive beautiful, cherished prizes that lift their hearts and give purpose and meaning to their lives.

As Xenophon in "The Estate Manager," a famous Greek classic on economy, explains, assets are "beneficial things" if they produce a profit or surplus as the prizes for human efforts. If a person owns horses, cattle, flocks, or money or possesses knowledge but does not know how to use these resources to increase his benefits, then all these assets become liabilities: "It follows that the same things are assets if one knows how to make use of them, and are not assets if one doesn't." People who are "unwillingly to do anything with their expertise," a manager who "incurs a loss through ignorance of how to make use of his flocks," or a person who misuses his money "to buy a concubine and consequently to damage his body, mind, and estate" all waste their resources and fail to increase their benefits. They win no prizes. For Xenophon persons, both friends and enemies, also are assets "if one knows how to make use of them, so as to derive benefit from them." He does not mean to exploit or manipulate them but to win the loyalty of friends through kind favors and to reconcile enemies through magnanimous deeds. In the dialogue between Socrates who lives a simple life with a modest income and Critobulus who possesses a fortune and lives a luxurious life, the rich man asks the poor man to manage his wealth because Socrates knows how to use assets to produce increase. Though Socrates owns "not even a hundredth" of the property of Critobulus, the rich man seeks his wise management "because I see that you know how to create a surplus."

Just like a farmer, merchant, or landowner who does not know how to use his assets to create benefits or "prizes" in the form of profits, surpluses, or abundance, a nation too can waste its resources and impoverish itself and its people through bad management. Recent American history illustrates the truth of Xenophon's ancient wisdom. The Iraq War has alienated America's friends and allies, and it has provoked her enemies— two potential assets. The war has emptied America's treasury and created enormous national debt through deficit spending, producing nothing of value or of future benefit. It has devastated a nation, reaped the deaths of over 5,000 Americans and tens of thousands of Iraqis, and left the country in the shambles of a wasteland. None of this wealth or effort has created a surplus. American and European families who do not replace themselves and who do not regard children as "assets" also bury their talents and fail to multiply. Of course the perversity and violence of legalized abortion in a culture of death defeat everything that Homer celebrates in the scenes of harvest and abundance and that Xenophon teaches in his economy of assets and surpluses in which a generous Mother Nature is ready to offer abundant fruits and great surpluses as inestimable prizes in exchange for man's respect for the natural and divine order of things. Agriculture, "the most generous art," as Xenophon describes it, rewards man with great harvests and plentiful surpluses, if man simply honors Nature's design and wisely uses the abundant assets that bless man. In Christ's teaching also, the workman who buries his talents and the tree that bears no fruit waste their assets and produce no prizes, thus frustrating God's plan and Mother Nature's design for man and the earth to be fruitful and multiply.

Chapter 10. The Manliness
of Chivalry

In Louisa May Alcott's *Little Men*, Mrs. Jo, who is both a mother figure and a headmistress at the Plumfield Academy for boys, testifies, "And I never saw the boy yet whom I could not get on capitally with after I had once found the soft spot in his heart." This "soft spot" is the gentleman or knight in each boy which education in the home and school awaken. One of the ways it manifests itself in the novel is the special protection and affection that Dan, the "firebrand" and strongest boy in the school, extends to Teddy, the smallest and most tender of the boys: "So Mrs. Jo soon saw and felt that there was a soft spot in rough Dan, and bided her time to touch and win him." Mrs. Jo recognizes that boys and men by nature desire the approval and admiration of the women they love. In how many homes and schools is this truth about human nature acknowledged?

In Thomas Hughes' *Tom Brown's School Days*, Dr. Arnold, the headmaster at Rugby famous for his doctrine of "muscular Christianity," welcomes the ordinary boys of rural England and educates and civilizes them to become Christian gentlemen committed to honor, principle, and moral courage. Learning that lying and bullying are incompatible with the ideal of "muscular Christianity" in the eternal battle of good and evil in the world, the Rugby boys learn fearlessness on the rugby field and in the moral arena. Through a series of trials and errors in which

Tom Brown fights older bullies and conquers his own bad moral habits, he learns the ignominy of cheating, cowardice, and tyranny and graduates as a leader with moral earnestness and the magnanimity of a gentleman, always putting justice above expediency and honor above popularity. In the cricket championship match that concludes the novel, Tom weighs the options of selecting a more talented player to bat or allowing a younger, more inexperienced player to have his turn in the game. Rather than winning at all costs, Tom values integrity above victory, reasoning "what a world of good" it would do for Arthur to be in the game. Like Plumfield Academy, Rugby School cultivates the knight and gentleman in all rough and tumble boys, appealing to their inherent nobility and idealism. Why have these ideals disappeared from public schools, colleges, and the culture at large?

The two knights in Chaucer's "The Knight's Tale," Palamon and Arcite, will fight to the death to win the hand of their beloved Emily, and Cervantes' Don Quixote will fast and do penance in the Sierra Morena Mountains as proof of his undying devotion to his peerless Lady Dulcinea del Toboso. Men have the potential for chivalry and sacrifice, willing to defend, serve, and honor women. Thus there is a "soft spot" in every boy's heart, a "little man" in every boy, "a Christian gentleman" in every Rugby student, a chivalrous knight in every lover, and a quixotic element in every man. Manhood in Western civilization has been imbued with this ideal through the manners of a gentleman, the pledge of knightly vows, military codes of honor, and educational philosophies concerned with character. Given man's essentially chivalric, noble nature, why has the modern world seen the demise of honor and magnanimity on the part of men, especially in the number of fatherless families?

In Howard Pyle's version of *The Merry Adventures of Robin Hood*, the Tanner sings a ballad entitled "The Wooing of Sir Keith" in which an old, ugly woman arrives at King Arthur's court begging for the noble deed of a chivalrous knight:

> "Quoth she, 'I have a foul disease
>   Doth gnaw my very heart,
> And but one thing can bring me ease
>   Or cure my bitter smart,
>
> " 'There is no rest, no ease for me
>   North, east, or west, or south,
> Till Christian knight will willingly
>   Three kiss me on the mouth.

After King Arthur, Sir Launcelot, Sir Tristram, and Sir Gawaine refuse to answer the "foulest dame's" request, Sir Keith volunteers to honor the hag's desperate plea and kisses her three times. Thereupon the foul dame is transformed into the fair maiden with the reddest of cheeks, the most fawn-like of eyes, and the most glittering of hair. This beautiful princess offers her love and wealth to the chivalrous Gawaine: "For never knight hath lady shown/ Such noble courtesy."

This motif of the handsome knight kissing the wizened hag appears in George MacDonald's *At he Back of the North Wind* in the fairy tale entitled "Little Daylight" in which a beautiful princess is plagued by an evil fairy's spell. The lovely maid dances only in the nighttime when no one beholds her beauty, and she is hidden in sleep during the daylight hours so that no one can love her. When a prince beholds her transformed into an old woman moaning as if dying, he lifts her in his arms and pities the old crone: " 'Mother, Mother!' said he. 'Poor mother!' and kissed her on the withered lips." Miraculously, the dying lady assumes the form of a lovely princess. Because he kissed Little Daylight when she was an old decrepit woman, she now kisses him in the form of a dazzlingly beautiful maiden whose countenance is as bright as the glorious son: "The prince recoiled in overmastering wonder. It was Daylight herself." Courtship, love, and marriage are inspired by chivalry and honor—the quintessential masculine virtues that capture a woman's heart and awaken her deepest love and gratitude. Why is this knightly ideal hardly in vogue in modern culture where the exploitation of women appears commonplace, especially in the habit of contraception, the practice of abortion, and the tolerance of cohabitation—all areas in which men commonly use women for pleasure, gain, or convenience?

In the above examples boys and men are taught and educated according to a masculine ideal founded on honor and generosity, a desire to please the women they love and act with noble, selfless motives. Mrs. Jo assumes that the male nature possesses an innate "soft spot" that exercises strength to protect the weak and please women. Her education of her "little men" at home and at school does not compromise the ideals of manhood. She does not lower her standards to the mediocrity of the lowest common denominator, to the "dumbing down" mentality that expects nothing of students besides minimum effort. When the boys act like boors at Daisy's party, they are punished by losing the favor of all female company for a week. Dr. Arnold's educational philosophy is also based on moral excellence. When Tom Brown acquires the reputation of a troublemaker because of violating rules and ignoring his studies, he is threatened with expulsion and given an ultimatum. Dr. Arnold's school requires will power, moral courage, and the habits of a Christian gentleman. The knightly code in Chaucer's tale and in *Don Quixote* is a venerable institution that Chaucer summarizes in his "General Prologue":

> There was among us a brave knight who had loved chivalry, truth, and honor, generosity and courtesy, from the time of his first horseback rides. (Modern English translation)

In all these works chivalry is unabashedly celebrated and affirmed.

Unlike the medieval culture of knighthood, the Christian ideals of manhood in Alcott's novel, and the muscular heroism exalted in Victorian England, the postmodern world denies or fails to teach the essentially noble, chivalric nature of man. Where feminist ideology prevails, egalitarianism replaces chivalry. If men and women are equal and the same with only biological differences, then women do not expect or inspire service; knights do not fight or sacrifice for women who are contemptuous of men or utterly independent as Palamon and Arcite do combat for their beloved Emily in Chaucer's tale. If patriarchy is the root of all evil and men are superfluous for the fulfillment of women as some feminists claim, then knighthood is an obsolete institution. As the natural, inherent distinctions between men and women diminish in military institutions and in the armed services, chivalry becomes redundant. Knighthood can flourish only when a culture clearly defines the meaning of masculinity and femininity. A gentleman knows that a woman deserves to be treated in special, considerate, sensitive ways that are reflected in manners, speech, and courtesy. If men and women look alike, dress alike, talk alike, and act alike, then the mysterious, idealistic, or romantic relationship between men and women disappears.

Knighthood also flourishes when women hold high ideals for men, expecting them to be magnanimous, gallant, civilized, and chaste. The ideals which women instill and expect in boys and men determine the moral level of a society. Do sex education courses, coeducational dormitories, or the easy availability of contraceptives in schools and campuses promote chivalry, the idealizing of women, or do they pander to lust, the exploiting of women for selfish pleasure? Without the virtue of chastity governing the relationships between men and women, the respect due to a woman's honor is absent. In Chaucer's "The Knight's Tale" Emily, the fair maiden the knights compete to win in marriage, is devoted to the Diana the goddess of chastity. Emily prays to her patroness:

> Behold, goddess of pure chastity, the bitter tears which fall upon my cheeks. Since you are a maid and the guardian of all maidens, guard and preserve my virginity, and as long as I live I will serve you as a maid.

Just as Emily inspires the gallantry and magnanimity of the knights, the virtue of chastity cultivates the ideal of chivalry. Likewise, modesty is the handmaiden of chastity. But how can modesty prevail in a pornographic culture where sexuality is flaunted in Hollywood, television, the mainstream media, and academic institutions?

The deadliest poison to chivalry, however, is contraception—the abuse of women's equilibrium and health through invasive devices and chemicals such as the Pill, Depo Provera, Norplant, and even RU-486. Instead of becoming elevated as a woman worthy of courtship, respect, dignity, and devotion in the way Palamon and Arcite honor Emily, fight to win her hand in marriage, and even risk death on her behalf, woman becomes, to quote from *Humanae Vitae*, "a mere instrument of selfish enjoyment," and no longer man's "respected and beloved companion." A chivalrous man gives with liberality; a contracepting man niggardly refuses the gift of self and total surrender, frustrating the fecund nature of love. A chivalrous man protects and defends woman; a contracepting man exposes a woman's health to many hazards, carelessly ignoring the many side-effects and potential dangers such as cervical cancer, liver cancer, heart attacks,, strokes, depression, migraines, and hair loss. A chivalrous man keeps his word, honors the truth, and is bound by the highest moral principles; a contracepting or sterilized man lies with his body language, pretending to give without really giving, and he avoids the truth that the act of love and the beginning of life are inseparable. A chivalrous man is thoughtful and courteous, respecting a woman's sensibilities and avoiding the giving of offense in thought, word, or deed. A contracepting man lacks tact and delicacy, assuming that contraception allows constant availability and instant gratification. Chivalry cannot thrive in a culture dominated by the contraceptive mentality where men are wont to take and use rather than serve, give, and sacrifice.

Thus the lack of education in the ideal of chivalry that reduces it to a relic of medievalism, the feminist rejection of the complementarity of the sexes that results in a unisex ideology, and the prevalence of a contraceptive mentality that divorces love from romance all reduce the mystery that governs the relationship between the sexes. What is that mystery? As the ballad of Sir Keith and the story of Little Daylight illustrate, when a man gives with a pure heart and makes a generous gift of himself in the manner of a noble knight, it transforms a woman. It makes her fall in love. It makes her want to surrender herself and long for marriage. It unlocks her heart, awakens her beauty, and inspires her to return love for love. It is woman's nature to love and give abundantly and totally, but that desire requires men to be noble gentlemen who respect her as a lady deserving of chivalry. Something dramatic and mysterious happens when the old hag changes into a beautiful princess and when Little Daylight is restored to life from nearly dying. A woman's heart melts, and the fullness of her femininity reveals itself. In both cases a handsome knight kisses an ugly crone, performing a disinterested act expecting nothing in return but the reward of loving good for its own sake. This kiss symbolizes the ultimate chivalric act of self-forgetfulness, honoring the woman for her own sake rather than for pleasure or gain. Woman intuitively senses when she is loved for her own sake and responds with all the gratitude, beauty, and generosity she possesses. This kind of love is dynamic and surprising, not perfunctory; a mutual giving and receiving in self-donation, not a hidden form of selfishness; a priceless gift, not a calculated risk.

This is the mystery of love that is lost in the sexual revolution that substitutes "safe sex" for true romance. When feminists resent masculinity, they stifle chivalry. When chastity is no longer valued as a moral norm, men do not idealize or respect women. The practice of contraception destroys the meaning of courtship in which men prove their love and worthiness and women feel desired because they are truly loved as persons. When education is reduced to the lowest common denominator and boys and girls are assumed to be "sexually active" rather than to be gentlemen and ladies, ideals such as honor or purity lose their credibility. Instead of romance leading to the wonder of the true, the good, and the beautiful that are incarnate in the beloved, the experience of love degenerates into the various forms of lust that are advertised as sexual liberation. Without chivalry men and women become dehumanized, and love loses its heart.

In Chaucer's tales the maxim that epitomizes the chivalric man is, "Pity runs quickly in gentle hearts." Knights are moved by the plights of women grieving for their dead husbands in battle who cry for mercy; they are touched by women in distress who cry for deliverance by men who feel compassion; they are melted by the heartfelt tears and anguish of women who are suffering. These women rely on the good hearts, noble sentiments, and magnanimous souls of real men—princes and knights like Palamon and Arcite, Sir Keith, and Don Quixote who will idealize them, fight for them, sacrifice for them, and even die for them. When women find such men, their bountiful hearts respond with the warmth, beauty, and splendor of total love and complete surrender.

What Louisa May Alcott and Thomas Arnold knew about human nature—the "soft spot" in a boy's heart, the gentleman in each boy, the Don Quixote in every man—the modern world eliminates by its preoccupation with "sexism". In a culture ridden by feminist ideology, the relations between the sexes become competitive, political, and exploitative. Love and romance lose their aura of mystery, and men and women do not make gifts of themselves to one another or to anyone else. While chivalry originates in the gentle or kind heart that puts woman first, sexual liberation puts self-gratification first and woman last. While chivalry evokes the princess or lady in a woman, the contraceptive mentality treats her as an object. While chivalry glories in the femininity of woman and in the idealism of love, unisex thinking reduces the meaning of sexuality to mere biological functions. Without chivalry informing the characters of men or influencing the education of boys, preparation for marriage suffers. "Husbands, love your wives," St. Paul enjoins, "as Christ also loved the church, and delivered himself up for it" (Ephesians 5: 25). A chivalrous man, in imitation of Christ, will love, sacrifice, and die for his wife and children. And a woman who is blessed with the Christ-like love of a noble husband will offer him her generous heart and understand perfectly St. Paul's injunction: "Wives, obey your husbands." Because the modern world debunks chivalry, it fails to grasp the mystery of love and the meaning of marriage which St. Paul illuminates by comparing the love between man and woman to the sacrificial love of Christ for his beloved.

Chapter 11. The Moral Imagination in the Classics of Children's Literature

The human body is clothed to reflect the dignity and glory of persons created in the image of God. While appropriate clothing in good taste expresses beauty, it also reveals goodness, for the beautiful, as St. Thomas Aquinas said, is "the attractive aspect of the good". Goodness radiates beauty, and beauty reflects goodness. Or as Henry Fielding writes in *Tom Jones*, one must not only *be* good in a moral sense but also *appear* to be good in proper dress. Beautiful appearances and attractive first impressions matter. Good morals express themselves in the clothing of pleasing manners, and Edmund Spenser depicted the virtue of civility in *The Faerie Queene* (Book VI) in the form of the three lovely Graces—mild Euphrosyne, fair Aglaia, and merry Thalia—who form a beautiful dance. While clothes represent the external, visible dimension of human nature, they also reflect the hidden and mysterious nature of persons, for the body manifests the soul. Because human nature is a unity of body and soul, physical beauty can mirror a good heart or the pure soul.

To be negligent of clothing, appearance, or manners is to hide a lamp under a bushel and not let the light shine out. To be deprived of dignified, beautiful clothing is to lose one's humanity, to be reduced to animals, and to be denied individuality. In Shakespeare's *King Lear*,

Lear's daughters Goneril and Regan insist that an older man and retired king who has divided his inheritance does not need a hundred retainers to attend him. Goneril asks, "What need you five and twenty, ten or five . . . ?" To Lear's daughter a former king's attendants have no practical function. Regan agrees that a king's followers serve no useful purpose when he no longer retains power: "What need one?" Offended and insulted at his daughters' attempts to rob him of his royal prerogatives, Lear vents his stern anger:

> Oh, reason not the need. Our basest beggars
> Are in the poorest things superfluous.
> Allow not nature more than nature needs,
> Man's life's as cheap as beasts. Thou art a lady.
> If only to go warm were gorgeous,
> Why, nature needs not what thou gorgeous wear'st,
> Which scarcely keeps thee warm.

As Lear explains, the purpose of clothing goes beyond protection and warmth. Even a beggar possesses articles of clothing which are not strictly necessary. Human beings dress for beauty and elegance, not for mere utility. The beautiful apparel of women bestows upon them a grace and elegance that corresponds with their femininity and rank. As a former king, Lear deserves the external symbols (clothing) of his office as testimony to his honor. Without the extra, unnecessary, "superfluous" accessories of clothing that elevate human beings, "man's life's as cheap as beasts" as Lear says: man would be indistinguishable from animals.

Because beauty and goodness are related and inseparable, the moral imagination in the children's classics depicts goodness as beautiful and attractive. The great books in children's literature do not depict goodness as something abstract, neutral, plain, or unappealing; rather goodness is powerfully real, full of wonder, vibrantly alive, and deeply moving. Goodness is charged with life, energy, and power. In the words of Simone Weil, "Imaginary evil is romantic and varied; real evil is gloomy, monotonous, barren, boring. Imaginary good is boring; real good is always new, marvelous, intoxicating." The moral imagination, then, portrays this exciting, adventurous aspect of real goodness by unifying goodness with beauty. The imagination vests goodness with attraction, charm, appeal, romance, and wonder. The imagery of goodness that makes it alluring and lovable corresponds to the clothing that adorns the human figure with dignity and lets the soul shine through the body.

The moral imagination is the faculty that allows children and adults to see goodness when it is dressed up—to see, hear, smell, feel, and taste goodness. Goodness is something sensory and vivid, not just conceptual and abstract. The moral imagination infuses a robust vitality and an invigorating spirit into the meaning of goodness to make it full of life and surprises—not some humdrum quality, ephemeral feeling, or vague generalization. The moral imagination selects from its wardrobe the clothing of metaphors, symbols, and pictures that radiate the splendor of goodness by impressing upon the mind and heart beautiful sights, memorable words, and living examples. Here are some examples of the moral imagination at work in the classics of children's literature: A boundless heart of love which never stops giving resembles a miraculous pitcher which replenishes itself when it is emptied. A good deed is like a buried seed that mysteriously ripens and bears abundant fruit in its special harvest time. The truth will always out and erupts in the most amazing, unforeseen way as elves, birds, and bees whisper it. Children, nursery rhymes, and fairy tales all have something in common. They are "windows" allowing an outside world to come in and permitting the mind to see beyond. Gold is not the wealth of King Midas who transforms everything into base metal but the riches of his child Marygold, more precious than all the world's treasure. These examples from children's literature capture the aura of glory and the natural fascination that the wonder of goodness evokes. Goodness by its nature is beautiful, and the moral imagination paints it in the most resplendent colors and elegant clothes.

In Nathaniel Hawthorne's tale "The Miraculous Pitcher" from *A Wonder Book,* the elderly couple of Baucis and Philemon practices the virtue of hospitality and honors a sacred law of the Greek gods. All travelers, regardless of their social status or material wealth, receive the same gracious welcome and partake of the hearty food that Baucis and Philemon generously offer to all guests. The couple never refuses a visitor and never stops giving from the abundance of their pure hearts. In the story two shabby vagabonds rejected by the villagers because of their miserable appearance find a cordial reception in the home of Baucis and Philemon: "'Friends,' said the old man, 'sit down and rest yourselves here on this bench. My good wife Baucis has gone to see what you can have for supper. We are poor folks;

but you shall be welcome to whatever we have in the cupboard.'" As Baucis serves her guests, she refills their cups of milk until she empties the pitcher with the last drop. To her astonishment Baucis notices that the two travelers continue to pour more milk from the empty pitcher: "What was her surprise, therefore, when such an abundant cascade fell bubbling into the bowl, that it was immediately filled to the brim and overflowed upon the table!" The elderly couple senses that they have entertained two Greek gods in disguise who will not be outdone in generosity. In gratitude for the bountiful hospitality they have received, the Greek gods bestow on Baucis and Philemon the gift of The Miraculous Pitcher which always refills upon being emptied to the last drop. After peeping into the pitcher and discovering "it contained not so much as a single drop," Philemon then "beheld a little white fountain, which gushed up from the bottom of the pitcher, and speedily filled it to the brim with foaming and deliciously fragrant milk." The image of goodness, then, is that of an overflowing fountain or outpouring cascade.

In this story the moral imagination equates goodness with the simple kindness of an elderly couple who are pure in heart. The story associates the natural appeal of Baucis and Philemon's goodness with the appetizing savory food she places on the table: homemade bread, slices of cheese, honey "of the purest and most transparent gold" with the fragrance of flowers, clusters of grapes "on the point of bursting with ripe juice," and deliciously fragrant milk from "the richest herbage that could be found anywhere in the world." The moral imagination pictures the goodness of the human heart as an abundant stream of never ending milk, as a miraculous pitcher that can never be depleted. The more love the heart gives, the more love the heart receives to give again. The pitcher must be emptied in order to be refilled. Baucis and Philemon give all and give their best to their guests, only to discover that they have received more than they gave. Thus the moral imagination portrays the irresistible charm of innocence and the natural magic of goodness. The beauty of the hospitable hearts of Baucis and Philemon touch and move the hearts of the Greek gods to say "An honest, hearty welcome to a guest works miracles with the fare, and is capable of turning the coarsest food to nectar and ambrosia." The moral imagination captures the excitement and romance of goodness—its spellbinding power to touch the human heart and to change common life into a beautiful adventure that resembles "turning the coarsest food to nectar and ambrosia". In this way "real good is always new, marvelous, intoxicating" as Simone Weil writes.

In Hans Andersen's "A Traveling Companion" the moral imagination presents goodness as a buried seed—a small, humble deed performed in the silence and darkness of the night. No one notices the good deeds of poor John toward strangers and in obscure places like graveyards. On a journey to seek his fortune, the young man takes shelter in a church during a stormy night where he beholds a dead body awaiting burial. Two rogues, however, are awaiting their opportunity to desecrate the body and exact their revenge on the dead man who never paid them his debts. To prevent this outrage, poor John parts with his last $50 and pays the dead man's debts to appease his persecutors: " 'I've only fifty dollars,' said John. 'It's the whole of my inheritance, but I'll give it to you willingly if you'll promise me faithfully to leave the poor man in peace.'" This good deed occurs in the stealth of the night, in the solitude of a graveyard, and in the company of strangers whom he will never see again. Poor John performs this charitable work and then forgets about it, never thinking of the episode again as he continues on his journey into the future. On his way he encounters a friendly man who becomes his "traveling companion" and joins him in his various adventures. When poor John—under penalty of death—must guess the answer to riddles to win the hand of the princess whom he loves, this traveling companion assists with extraordinary help and saves John's life. He overhears the correct answers and knows the magical formula of how to transform a wicked witch into a lovely princess. Overwhelmed with gratitude and attributing all his happiness to the friendship of his traveling companion, John learns the mystery of his fellow traveler. The mysterious friend explains:

> I have only paid my debt. Do you remember the dead man those wicked men wanted to harm? You gave all you had so that he could lie quietly in his grave. I am that dead man.

The good deed in the graveyard performed long ago and forgotten resembles the tiny buried seed that now bears fruit. What appeared dead in the past returns to life in the future. A small, unnoticeable gesture of kindness yields a cornucopia of blessings. The good deeds sown in the past yield a bountiful harvest at some unforeseen moment in the future. In his humility poor John took no pride in his virtue, performed good by stealth, and loved goodness for its sake and as its own reward. Never assuming that others were beholden to him, poor John never expected rewards or repayments, but he was blessed beyond his wildest dreams or expectations. Great events originate in small beginnings and humble origins. A person's past actions—for good or for ill—follow him and return to him at some point in the future in the ripeness of time. The moral imagination, then, creates a picture of goodness as potent, fruitful, and life-giving, for an act of kindness resurrects the dead man from his grave.

The moral imagination again illuminates the romance and adventure of goodness, the splendor of its glory. Poor John who began his journey with a meager $50 which he spent to pacify the vengeful men vandalizing the dead body travels penniless, but he deposits good deeds on the way that lie hidden and buried—seeds that burst into abundant fruit. The potentiality of a simple good deed is immeasurable; the seeds of goodness are potent and fecund as the bounty of the reaping exceeds the labor of the sowing. John's pure, generous heart produces life-changing events: life comes out of death as the dead man in the church becomes the lively traveling companion, good comes out of evil as the wicked witch changes into the lovely princess, and the penniless John acquires the wealth of the kingdom as he marries the princess. Thus goodness is dynamic, dramatic, creative, and wild with surprises—a life of great adventure, not humdrum blandness. To clothe goodness with the picture of something small becoming something great, someone humble becoming exalted, and something forgotten being remembered is to invest it with the wonder of the miraculous. Once again true goodness is "new, marvelous, intoxicating," beautiful to behold and not dressed in rags.

In Hawthorne's "The Golden Touch" King Midas's jaded imagination envisioned the gold of money as the essence of true beauty and the rarest form of goodness: "If ever he happened to gaze for an instant at the gold-tinted clouds of sunset, he wished that they were real gold, that they could be squeezed safely into his strongbox." When his daughter brought him buttercups and dandelions, he remarked, "If these flowers were as golden as they look, they would be worth the plucking!" When a Greek god finally grants Midas the magical power of the golden touch, his wish comes true. The spectacles, the book, the roses, the food, and his daughter Marygold all turn to gold metal. Unable to see the beauty of the natural world, to read the wisdom in books, to enjoy the fragrance of the roses, to taste the deliciousness of food, or to delight in the irresistible charm of his daughter's smile because Midas's golden touch has robbed them of their goodness and beauty, Midas soon repents his choice. His defective moral imagination envisioned the goodness, beauty, and wonder of natural blessings as monotonous and boring and exaggerated the gold of money as ultimate goodness and glorious beauty. Abounding in the luxurious wealth of gold coin but deprived of the simple pleasures of sight, taste, smell, and love, Midas laments, "And I have lost all that my heart really cared for." A glass of water, a crust of bread, and the smile on his daughter's face are now "worth all the gold on earth". Blind to the wonders of the true blessings in his life, Midas valued the lifeless objects of gold more than the precious gifts of goodness, beauty, and love that comprised the true wealth of life.

In Hawthorne's story the moral imagination depicts the simple, natural pleasures of life as true gold, as precious value, as heavenly gifts. As Midas says of his daughter, "I would not have given that one small dimple in her chin for the power of changing this whole big earth into a solid lump of gold!" After realizing his fatal mistake, Midas never again conceives of the daily blessings of life as stale or commonplace but regards them as exquisite and rare. The hot pancakes, brook trout, boiled eggs, and fragrant coffee lose their ordinary quality and assume the nature of natural marvels as does his daughter: " 'My precious, precious Marygold!' cried he." The moral imagination, then, pictures goodness as priceless treasure, as enticing as the delicious breakfast Midas sacrificed when the golden touch changed food into metal, and as beautiful as the golden hair of Marygold and the flowers in his garden, "in which grew the biggest and beautifullest and sweetest roses that any mortal ever saw or smelt."

Thus the moral imagination is the art of choosing beautiful clothing—the right picture, the perfect image— to let the body reveal the soul, to allow the physical to manifest the spiritual, and to permit the natural to mirror the supernatural. As St. Paul said, "The invisible things of God are known by the things which are visible," and as St. Thomas Aquinas wrote, "There is nothing in the intellect which does not first come through the senses." Goodness needs to be clothed in beautiful colors and with tasteful wardrobe to exert its greatest appeal and to accomplish its greatest good. Goodness is not plain but resplendent, and its attractiveness captures the heart and moves the senses. As Plato said of virtue, anyone who beheld her would instantly fall in love. All good and great writers see this natural association between goodness and beauty and recognize that the good radiates a light, creates an atmosphere, and weaves a magical spell. This is no doubt what artists had in mind in creating haloes around saints. Their art involves the business of clothing—finding the right images and pictures, evoking the right senses and impressions, and creating the perfect models that will capture the essence of goodness, its sight, sound, smell, taste, and touch. Thus the moral imagination speaks to the whole person, body and soul, and cultivates what Edmund Burke called "the moral sentiments"—the knowledge of good and evil—"which the heart owns, and the understanding ratifies, as necessary to *cover* the defects of our naked shivering nature" (italics added). In other words, these "moral sentiments"—hospitality, friendship, courtesy, chivalry, honor—are the clothing which exalt human beings with dignity and divinity. The beauty of goodness moves the heart and stirs the feelings which Burke calls "the moral sentiments".

Although a healthy moral imagination sees goodness as beautiful and attractive and evil as ugly and repulsive, a corrupted moral imagination regards evil or folly as fascinating and exciting and equates goodness with the namby-pamby, dull, or uninteresting. Just as King Midas's moral imagination saw gold metal as more precious than divine gifts, the emperor's daughter in Hans Andersen's "The Swineherd" disregards the most beautiful offerings of love and prefers the cheap to the precious, the trivial to the excellent. A prince brings rare gifts to the emperor's daughter to symbolize his great love: a rose that bloomed only once in five years "which smelled so sweetly that its scent would make one forget all one's sorrows and troubles" and a nightingale "which could sing as if all the beautiful melodies in the world were to be found in its throat." However, the emperor's daughter, seeing nothing exceptional, scorns the two choicest gifts and rejects the chivalrous love of the prince. When a swineherd (the prince in disguise) appears later with the novelty of a magical saucepan that detects "every dinner that was being cooked in every fire-place in the town," the daughter prefers this curious oddity with its ordinary smells to the rare rose with its exquisite perfume. Preferring the new to the old, the emperor's daughter gives the lowly swineherd ten kisses for a cheap item but despises the precious tokens of love generously offered. Likewise, the emperor's daughter chooses a silly rattle over the heavenly nightingale because the rattle produces the popular music of the day, "all the waltzes, barn-dances, and polkas that have ever been known since the creation of the world"—a sound that pleases her more than the haunting melodies of the bird's thrilling voice. Lacking a well-formed moral imagination, the daughter fails to appreciate the rose and the nightingale's great goodness and exceptional beauty. Although the goodness of the gifts expresses the pure love of the prince, the daughter ignores the intrinsic worth and the symbolic significance of the prized gifts. By condescending to purchase these trinkets with the coin of kisses, she pays dearly for junk with the best part of herself and despises the heavenly gifts of transcendent beauty. As Edmund Burke explained in *Reflections on the Revolution in France*, when a person lacks a moral imagination, "a king is but a man; a queen is but a woman; a woman is but an animal." For the emperor's daughter, the rose that blooms once in five years with the sweetest fragrance is just a mere flower, and the nightingale with the most beautiful of voices is just another common bird. Without a moral imagination everything is leveled, flattened, and one-dimensional.

While the cultivated moral imagination regards outward beauty as a sign of inward goodness or intrinsic worth and adorns goodness with the most attractive apparel, the stunted moral imagination strips away the outer garments or fails to choose appropriate elegant attire for the king, queen, or woman. Just as King Midas robbed flowers, food, and children of their essence—the miracle of their wonder—the emperor's daughter too reduces the glorious to the worthless and the precious to the cheap. The emperor's daughter illustrates the view of "imaginary good as boring" that Simone Weil mentioned—a modern view that appears in the whole trend called deconstruction, that is, the stripping away of grandeur, heroism, awe, and holiness from all the splendors of the past so that all that remains of goodness is the unsavory image of extremism. The classics are no longer great books but examples of sexism, racism, and prejudice. Marriage and the family are no longer sacred institutions rooted in nature and God but arbitrary, man-made arrangements subject to innovation. In other words, everything transcendent which exalts and uplifts must be debunked, reduced, and purged of its glory so that all traces of beauty are expunged and what remains is blandness and flatness. As Winston observes in Orwell's *1984*, "It struck him that the truly characteristic thing about modern life was not its cruelty and insecurity, but simply its bareness, its dinginess, its listlessness."

All true art transforms the quality of daily life and human experience so that it does not remain bare, dingy, or drab. It performs this alchemy—not by changing the structure of reality or painting the cheap or the ugly with bright colors—but by letting the light shine out from the truly good and beautiful, by releasing the form from matter as Michelangelo did when he said "There's a David in that hunk of rock." The moral imagination sees the king in the man, the queen in the woman, the wonder of the child, the beauty of the rose, and the miracle of the nightingale and then clothes these realities with symbols and images that illuminate the full glory they naturally possess. King Lear needs his one hundred retainers; a queen needs her royal apparel; true love needs its roses; King Midas needs his flower garden, not his gold pieces; every person needs clothing that reflects the image of God; and every touch of goodness needs to be beautiful inwardly and outwardly so that what *is* truly good also *appears* to be beautiful and its light shines out instead of remaining hidden under a bushel.

Chapter 12. St. Monica:
Mother, Wife, and Homemaker
as Saint

A person can measure his happiness and success in terms of public acclaim and renowned achievements or in terms of personal enrichment and humble deeds. A person can measure his life in terms of quantifiable results such as income, honors, victories, or publications or in terms of intangible criteria such as the love one brings to others or the lives one touches. A person can judge the quality of his life according to worldly standards or according to the ideals of the saints. A person can live in the limelight and on a grand scale or follow St. Therese of Lisieux's "little way" of obscurity and self-forgetfulness. A person can live in simplicity and do one thing well or live in multiplicity and do many things poorly. A person can live in a state of grace and bring peace and gladness to others or live in a state out of grace and become a burden to everyone. The character and life of Monica epitomize an ideal of sainthood essential for a modern world suffering a crisis of the family and the deconstruction of the home.

In the *Confessions* Augustine's autobiography presents the lives of three saints. While narrating the famous story of his conversion from Manichaeism to Christianity, Augustine not only remembers the profound influence of St. Ambrose's holy example and moving eloquence but also records the sanctity of his mother's life. While Augustine and Ambrose assumed public positions of prominence as eminent teachers and as great church fathers, Monica lived her entire life in the domestic realm as obedient daughter, dutiful wife, loving mother, and kind friend. While Augustine and Ambrose earned the title of bishop and addressed multitudes through their gifts of writing and speaking, Monica's sphere of influence was modest and humble. She waged no intellectual wars with the Manichaeans and never wrote on the doctrine of the Trinity, but Monica's stature is as great as the reputations of the golden-tongued bishop of Milan and the intellectually gifted bishop of Hippo. What is the secret of her sainthood?

Monica was true to her marital vocation and fulfilled all the duties of daughter, wife, mother, and friend. Augustine, writes, "For she had been the wife of one man, had requited her parents, had governed her house piously, was well reported of for good works, had brought up children, as often travailing in birth of them as she saw them straying away from you" (Book IX). Her home was a shrine of charity and always reflected the personal, sensitive touch of the feminine sensibility: "... she gave to each one of us the care that a mother gives to her son and to each one of us the service which a daughter gives to her father" (Book IX). Her example as gentle wife and calm peacemaker inspired and instructed other women in their marital problems, for she always avoided quarreling with her husband Patricius, notorious for his fiery temper: "But my mother knew that an angry husband must not be contradicted, not in deed nor even in word." After his rage was spent, she calmly reasoned with Patricius "if he had happened to fly into a rage for no good reason." She influenced and conquered her husband through her femininity, not only overcoming his irrational anger but even motivating his conversion to the Christian faith. Her advice to her married friends who complained of their husbands' violent behavior was "that the fault was in their tongues." Amazed and incredulous that the choleric Patricius had never struck Monica and that their quarrels never caused rancor, the women who followed her advice thanked her for her wisdom. Monica was never too busy or too preoccupied with her own domestic situation so as not to offer her friendship and counsel to other women. She sensed the needs of others and won the hearts of many women by her true friendship and good will.

Monica's special genius for mediation and peacemaking went beyond her own immediate domestic circle. She not only created harmony in her own household and negotiated domestic tranquility in other families but also mediated between quarrelsome friends. She possessed the great prudence and exquisite tact of holding her tongue, never resorting to gossip or tale-bearing and always remaining the perfect confidante. Augustine writes of his mother, "She might hear many bitter things said on both sides, and this kind of outpouring of swelling and undigested malice is very likely to take place when a woman talks to a friend who is present about an enemy who is absent.... But my mother would never report to one woman what had been said about her by another except insofar as what had been said might help to bring the two together." A discreet woman, she never repeated the uncharitable comments of others, thus exemplifying the beatitude, "Blessed are the peacemakers: for they shall be called the children of God." She mastered the art of reconciling people, living at peace with her choleric husband, teaching other married couples to live in harmony, and reuniting alienated friends. And as Augustine testfies, her intercessory prayers and constant petitions for his salvation converted him from Manichaeism to Christianity: "Could you refuse your help to her or despise her tears with which she asked from you, not gold or silver or any mutable and transitory good, but the salvation of her son's soul? .... No, Lord you could not." Thus as wife, mother, and friend Monica found the time to serve the primary needs of others. Generous with her time to her friends, sensitive to the marital problems suffered by others, and prudent in her conduct and advice, Monica performed many spiritual works of mercy in a quiet, unobtrusive way.

The role of a homemaker and housewife, then, is not confined to cooking, cleaning, and shopping. As full-time wife and mother Monica touched lives and moved hearts. She was all things to all people—a spiritual director to friends, an advocate for her son, a holy influence upon her husband, a mediator in disputes. Centered in the home, Monica exerted a maternal, feminine, womanly influence that civilizes the world. Augustine writes, "She was also the servant of your servants," for no one was too insignificant, no matter too trivial, and no task too demeaning for her life of Christian service. She transformed the environment around her from one of animosity and recrimination to one of peace and reconciliation. The temper of Patricius turned to meekness; the disobedience of Augustine changed to submission; the nagging, gossiping, uncharitable tongues of women learned to restrain their voices. Her charity was not limited only to her own immediate family but embraced all whom she knew, for "she gave to each one of us the care a mother gives to her son and to each one of us the service which a daughter gives to her father." She performed all these good works in the most natural, unassuming, and unofficious manner, as the normal extension of a wife and mother's normal duties within the home.

What was the secret of this humble woman's powerful influence? Addressing God, Augustine comments that "on the evidence of the fruit of her holy conversation they could feel your presence in her heart." It was not Monica's eloquence or rhetoric but her "holy conversation" that was the source of grace. Unlike the cultivated oratory of Ambrose or the learned discourses of Augustine, Monica's speech manifested the reality of God in the simplest and most personal of ways : *"cor ad cor loquitur"* (heart speaks to heart). She did not address large audiences or numbers of students but intimate friends and close family members. "Holy conversation" requires sincerity, charity, and trust—a concern for the true happiness of the other person, an obligation to speak the truth in giving advice, and confidentiality in respecting a person's privacy. Monica reflected the presence of God through the goodness of her heart. Augustine writes, "I remembered how devoutly and with what holiness she conducted herself in your sight, how kind and considerate she was to us." In short, Monica gave her heart to God, and God made her heart Christ-like in its giving. Bringing gifts daily to God's altar and requesting of Augustine before her death "that wherever you may be you will remember me at the altar of God," Monica gave to others what Christ gave to her, His burning furnace of love. Augustine marveled at the depth of his mother's love for him and the breadth of her love for relatives and neighbors. Whether it was her obedience to her parents, her long-suffering in enduring her husband's infidelities, "her patience and forbearance" toward her mother-in-law, or her forgiveness of others ("I know that she dealt mercifully and from her heart forgave her debtors their debts"), Monica imitated Christ's sacred heart and manifested it in her relations with family and neighbors in her duties as mother, wife, and friend.

Monica most naturally fulfills this most important work of bringing God to others in her marital vocation. Rather than preaching holiness or practicing apologetics, Monica attracts souls to God by the purity of her heart. Referring to his pagan father's conversion to the Catholic faith, Augustine (addressing God) writes, "She tried to win him to you by the beauty of the character which you had given her and by which you made her able to provoke love and respect and the admiration of her husband. Like her "holy conversation" this beauty of her character moved the hard-hearted and melted those who resisted God's grace. The genius of Monica's lovable, irresistible nature lies in her many simple deeds of charity and mercy—the promptness of her myriad good works performed in humility and obscurity in her small domestic circle. Like St. Therese of Lisieux, Monica practiced also "the little way," the performing of the smallest acts of kindness and favors that St. Therese calls "strewing flowers," that is, "not allowing one little sacrifice to escape, not one look, one word, profiting all by the smallest things and doing them through love." This "little way" St. Therese compares to perfuming the royal throne with "sweet scents" and singing in silvery tones "the canticle of Love." In other words, the beauty of goodness captures the heart and ravishes the soul.

Augustine's reference to his mother as "the servant of servants" and his comment "how kind and considerate she was to us" honor Monica for her mastery of "the little way," the sensitive acts of special thoughtfulness that unveil the beauty of the human heart. This "little way," however, abounds in great love, for as St. John of the Cross (quoted by St. Therese in *Story of a Soul*) writes, "the smallest act of PURE LOVE is of more value . . . than all other works together." This ideal of pure love by way of the smallest acts Monica embodies in her role of mother, wife, and friend. What St. Therese wrote of her mother also perfectly describes the beauty of the character of Augustine's mother: "Ah! How delicate a Mother's heart really is, and how it shows its tenderness in a thousand little cares that no one thinks about."

Therese's ideal of the "little way," St.John of the Cross's teaching about "the smallest acts of PURE LOVE," and the beauty of the delicate heart that busies itself "in a thousand little cares" illuminate the mystery of Monica's sanctity and the vocation of motherhood. Women who follow Monica's humble way as "the servant of servants" and worry about the thousand little things demanded in family life and human relationships cannot function in the dual roles of homemaker and professional careerist. The flourishing of Monica's womanly, motherly genius requires her to reign in the home. She cannot be diverted or distracted by economic pressures to provide a second income or by society's influence to pursue self-fulfillment. In the kingdom of the home she rules as queen with a sovereignty that addresses itself to the deepest of human needs and devotes itself to the most primary of human relationships: creating a peace-filled,hospitable home, forming the conscience of her son, honoring the vows of marriage, and being a source of grace and wisdom to other women. In her classic, *Gift From the Sea*, Ann Morrow Lindbergh writes of this traditional Christian role of woman:

> I want a singleness of eye, a purity of intention, a central core to my life that will enable me to carry out these obligations and activities as well as I can. I want, in fact—to borrow from the language of the saints—to live "in grace" as much of the time as possible. . . . I would like to achieve a state of inner spiritual grace from which I could function and give as I was meant to in the eye of God.

Monica's life testifies to her "singleness of eye"—her utmost concern for the salvation of her son's soul, the conversion of her husband, and her fidelity to God. Her life also affirms "a purity of intention," a virtue immediately recognized by the priest who reassured Monica in the midst of her tears for her wayward son that "As you live, it is impossible that the son of these tears should perish." Likewise, Monica cultivated "a central core" to her life that nourished all her human relationships and strengthened her in her sufferings. This "central core" she found in her daily visits to the church where Monica ". . . so constant in almsgiving, so willing and ready in the service of your saints . . . never let a day pass without making her oblation at your altar, who used to go, twice a day, without any exception, in the morning and in the evening, to your church . . . that she might listen to you in the sermons preached and that you might listen to her as she prayed." Because of this singleness of eye, purity of intention, and central core of Christian faith, Monica lived in that "state of inner spiritual grace" that she reflected in her holy conversation and in the beauty of her lovable character. As Augustine remarked, "All of them who knew her found good reason to praise and honor and love you, because on the evidence of the fruit of her holy conversation they could feel your presence in her heart." As mother, wife, and friend Monica touched and enriched the lives of all who remembered her.

Her genius as woman made others feel special. In describing God's tender, merciful, sensitive love for each person, Augustine—who discovered God's goodness in the loving heart of his mother—describes God's inestimable love for each human being as the most personal of all relationships, as if each person felt like the favorite son or darling daughter of his father: ". . . O omnipotent Good, you who care for each one of us as though he was your only care and who cares for all of us as though we were all just one person." Monica's special, unconditional love for her son communicated to Augustine the nature of God's familiar, intimate for each soul. In short, Monica's associations with friends and family members represent what Ann Morrow Lindberg calls "the pure relationship," "the magical closed circle," "the miraculous sense of two people existing only for the sake of each other." Paraphrasing Auden's famous line ("But to be loved alone"), Lindberg captures the quintessential meaning of feeling special and knowing personal love: "We all wish to be loved alone." Of course this ideal of the pure relationship is not selfish desire but the human heart's deepest longing for intimacy and communion with another. Monica and Augustine experienced this "magical closed circle" of true oneness in the garden of Ostia before her death when Monica opened the depths of her heart: "There was only one reason why I wanted to stay a little longer in this life, and that was that I should see you a Catholic Christian before I died. Now God has granted me this beyond my hopes." Women who value marriage as a vocation especially are endowed with this gift of making all those whom they love and care for feel special.

However, when woman is removed from the home, her influence as mother, wife, friend, and confidante wanes. She is less able to offer her "holy conversation" and wisdom to others and more restricted in attending to the thousand cares that require a woman's exquisite touch. Woman in the work force becomes too preoccupied and busy to think of what St. Therese calls "the smallest acts of PURE LOVE" or to follow "the little way." There is not enough time to cultivate those "pure relationships" of delighting in the presence, company, and friendship of others. The leisure and freedom do not exist to make others feel especially beloved. Hence Lindberg speaks of "certain environments, certain modes of life" that are "more conducive to inner and outer harmony than others," but overwork undermines this inner peace that creates wholeness and a sense of being "in grace." She warns of the endless distractions that create the "multiplicity that the wise men warn us of.": "It leads not to unification but to fragmentation. It does not bring grace; it destroys the soul." Thus in a culture that worships work, encourages two-income families, and measures a woman's worth by her career and profession, mothers and wives are not easily disposed to be their true womanly selves in the fullest sense. "Woman instinctively wants to give, yet resents giving herself in small pieces," Lindberg writes. But modern conditions discourage the kind of self-donation and total giving that Monica's life personifies. Instead, as Brian C. Robertson's *There's No Place Like Work* explains, the pursuit of wealth replaces the saint's "little way":

> Society has taught us to trade in those apron strings of motherhood and housewifery for power suits, running shoes, and pagers, all in the name of equal rights and financial success. This culminates in the idea that prevails in this monetary world today, whereby "more is more."

When work replaces home as the primary arena of a woman's life, the Monicas have little time to care for the spiritual and emotional needs of their children, few occasions to create the harmonious atmosphere of a home, and no free moments to attend to those "thousand little cares" and "pure acts of love" that create a human life. Women like Monica for whom family comes first are the saints of modern civilization who will restore the civilization of love to the culture of death.

Chapter 13. The Sufferings
of the Wanderer

The experience of the wanderer is a great affliction that wearies the human spirit and robs human life of its joy, purpose, and meaning. The fate of the wanderer refers not only to the homeless, rootless traveler lost at sea or exiled in foreign lands but also to the restless thinker or skeptical intellectual who never seeks, discovers, loves, or defends the truth. In the Old English poem "The Wanderer," a lonely mariner weary of endless miles of ocean and travel yearns for the heartwarming comforts of his familiar home and dearest family members. In Homer's *Odyssey* the heroic Odysseus, exiled for nine years on the island of the goddess Calypso, mourns day and night for his beloved wife, son, and father in Ithaca as he walks the beaches of the island in a state of perpetual melancholy: "Life with its sweetness was ebbing away in the tears he shed for his lost home. . . . But the days found him sitting on the rocks or sands, torturing himself with tears and groans and heartache, and looking out with streaming eyes across the watery wilderness."

St. Augustine in the *Confessions* also lamented his tortured soul and intellectual darkness as he dabbled with the various schools of philosophy and heresies of the ancient world, frustrated and disillusioned by the Skeptics, the Subverters, the astrologists, and the Manichees: "O you infinite mercy, my God, my refuge from those terrible destroyers, among whom I wandered with a stiff neck on my path further and further away from you, loving my own ways and not yours, loving the liberty of a runaway." In Boethius's *The Consolation of Philosophy* Lady Philosophy berates Boethius's immoderate sorrow and excessive anger at the fickleness of fortune that has robbed him of his worldly status. She reprimands her illustrious student for losing his way: "You have wandered away yourself; you too have deserted for a while your usual calm," adding "you ought to bear with equanimity whatever happens on Fortune's ground." At the beginning of his journey in the *Divine Comedy*, Dante also feels disoriented and confused in his aimless wandering: "Midway in our life's journey, I went astray/ from the straight road and woke to find myself/ alone in a dark wood" (I, I, 1-3; Ciardi translation). What is this state of mind, body, and soul that afflicts the wanderers of the earth and the wanderers of the mind?

Emotionally starved for the bonds of family and for the affections of the home, the wanderer lacks a human life. The wanderers in the *Odyssey* are merely struggling to survive, not enjoying the happiness of living life to its fullest. Escaping from cruel enemies, haunted by the threat of hunger, and alienated from their native land, they beg to return to civilization, to be a member of a society or a household, and to live a life of stability. The wanderers in Homer's epic do not plant and sow, and they do not reap the harvest of life, the fruitfulness of marriage and the joy of the homecoming that Homer associates with the return of Odysseus to Ithaca to be reunited in love with his wife, son, and father—a sowing and reaping that Homer captures in the image of father and son planting fruit trees in the vineyard when Laertes held Odysseus by the hand: "I was only a little boy at the time, trotting after you through the orchard, begging for this and that, and as we wound our way through these very trees you told me all their names." The wanderer's restless life, then, never allows him to take roots, to love and to be loved, and to complete the circle of life in which parents behold the happy marriages of their children and children repay their parents for their loving care. The loyal swineherd Eumaeus summarizes the lot of the wanderer he formerly suffered: "Surely a tramp's life is the worst thing that anyone can come to. Yet exile, misfortune, and sorrow often force a man to put up with its miseries for his wretched stomach's sake." To be a wanderer is not to live a human life.

The life of intellectual wandering also brings misery to a human life as St. Augustine's autobiography testifies. Both in his actual travels from Carthage to Rome to Milan and in his intellectual journeys, Augustine lived a restless life in which worldly gain and sensual pleasures failed to gratify the deepest hungers of his mind, heart, and soul. Recalling "all those wanderings of my error in the past," Augustine traveled in a maze that led to nothing but constant unhappiness: "I could not rest. I could not think intelligently. . . . And myself to myself had become a place of misery, a place where I could not bear to be and from which I could not go." Just as the wanderer on sea and land seeks the haven of the home to alleviate the desolation of loneliness, the mind also hungers for its own natural "home"—the truth—to curb its restless meandering. As Augustine's famous statement indicates, the wandering mind that never rests in the truth resembles the vagabond always looking for a home to begin his life: "you have made us for yourself, and our hearts are restless until they can find peace in you." Just as the wanderer on earth never participates in the great plan of Mother Nature's law, the giving and receiving of love in the sowing and reaping of love's fruitfulness in marriage, family, and children, the wanderer in the realm of truth—constantly deceived—also never feels a sense of belonging or enjoys "life with its sweetness."

As Augustine's constant coming and going in the world of philosophical errors illustrates, evil is legion, and its fruits are bitter, not sweet. False doctrines and heresies abound to accommodate the life of sin which requires rationalization and the removal of guilt. Whether it is astrology that denies the moral responsibility of choice, Manichaeism that attributes sin to the god of darkness rather than to the corrupt will of man, or the Skeptics that deny the existence of truth or man's capacity for discovering it, the wandering mind that travels in circles or thrives in constant change not only never discovers the truth but also never knows the reality of goodness, beauty, and God—the transcendentals of classical philosophy known as the One, the True, the Good, and the Beautiful. In other words, the wandering mind's view of ultimate reality remains confined to the physical, the material, and the temporal. None of the pleasures of the world satisfied Augustine's wandering mind that thought of happiness only in terms of the gratification of the body: "There was no rest for it—anywhere—not in pleasant groves, not in games and singing, not in sweet-smelling gardens, not in fine banquets, not in the pleasures of the bed, not in the reading of books, nor in poetry." To wander with the mind is to substitute a false doctrine for a true belief.

To wander, then, is to search without finding, to work without achieving—a form of futility that Solomon expresses in his famous cry of "Vanity of Vanities," the useless effort that always leads to failure illustrated by the myth of Sisyphus forever rolling his rock up the hill. The sense of wandering always conveys a sense of purposeless or meaningless repetition that never reaches any goal. In the world of the dead in the *Odyssey* the disembodied spirits hover throughout the realm of Hades searching to make contact with the living, only to be frustrated for their efforts. When Odysseus stretches his arms to embrace his deceased mother, "like a shadow or a dream, she slipped through my arms and left me harrowed by an even sharper pain." This life of wandering in the lower world moves Achilles to proclaim, "Put me on earth again, and I would rather be a serf in the house of some landless man . . . than king of all these dead men that have done with life." Augustine experiences a similar state of mind as a result of his intellectual wanderings when he rails against the fornication of the mind—the sophistry of rationalization and deceit, the abuse of the intellect for purposes for which it was never intended by nature and by God. He addresses God, "you I did not love. Against you I committed fornication, and in my fornication I heard all around me the words: 'Well done! Well done!'" Just as man is intended to belong to a family, participate in a society, and cooperate with Mother Nature's design, so also the human mind is designed to know the truth and contemplate God's goodness and love. The aimless traveler and the wandering mind act contrary to nature, the traveler never establishing a home and the intellect never resting in the truth. To travel and go no place, to think and to know nothing does not make any sense of a human life and a human mind.

Boethius in *The Consolation of Philosophy* also let his mind stray from the heights of wisdom. Formerly a scholar eminent for his vast learning and a distinguished Roman consul honored by Theodoric and the Emperor of Constantinople for his public service, Boethius is shocked by a tragic fall from high to low as he awaits his unjust death sentence in prison. From the heights of worldly glory he now finds himself without titles, honor, wealth, or happiness. Accused by Lady Philosophy of a loss of self-possession and equanimity, Boethius in his ignorance attributes the loss of his former happiness to the power of fickle Fortune and denies the sovereignty of God's Divine Providence in governing the irrational whims of Fortune's mutability. The teacher reprimands her pupil for the failure to exercise man's "godlike quality in virtue of his rational nature," arguing, "You cannot impose anything on a free mind, and you cannot move from its state of inner tranquility a mind at peace with itself and firmly founded on reason." In Boethius's case the wandering mind is not tempted by the world, the flesh, and the devil as in Augustine's example but by excessive anger and immoderate sorrow in the emotional overreaction to misfortune. The wandering mind loses sight of the true source of human happiness and imagines the gifts of Fortune—power, riches, glory, and pleasure—to be the *summum bonum*. Lady Philosophy calls these worldly benefits "false happiness" and explains that "these roads to happiness are side-tracks and cannot bring us to the destination they promise."

The wandering mind, then, confuses true happiness and false happiness as it identifies fickle Fortune as the source of all true good and fails to see that the spiritual, not the temporal, is the happiness it seeks: "goodness is happiness"—a happiness that begins and ends in God and a "self-sufficiency" man attains independently of Fortune when the divine reason in man—the image of God—acts according to its nature and masters the passions with self-possession. The "side-tracks" represent the places where Boethius has strayed, travels to places that do not possess the object of his desires: "Alas, how men by blindness led/ Go from the path astray./ Who looks on spreading boughs for gold,/ On vines for jewels gay?" Instead of gazing outward at the favors of Fortune for the blessings of happiness, Boethius is instructed to look within at his own rational capacity and moral powers: "Why then do you mortal men seek after happiness outside yourselves, when it lies within you?" According to Lady Philosophy's judgment, Boethius has forgotten "his true nature"—his godlike, divine mind that transcends the vicissitudes of Fortune's erratic nature: "It seems as if you feel a lack of any blessing of your own inside you, which is driving you to seek your blessings in things separate and external." In short, Boethius's wandering mind lets the passions enslave reason instead of exercising the freedom of the mind "made in the image of God" to master the emotions. Without the medicine of truth or the strength of wisdom, the mind remains easily misled into the wrong paths that lead to a sense of betrayal because of Fortune's deception. To wander with the mind never leads to true happiness because ignorance never produces the equanimity of wisdom.

In the *Divine Comedy* Dante also needs direction to lead him out of the "dark wood" back to the "straight road" from which he wandered. Lost in "so arduous a wilderness," he finds himself at a loss to explain when "I first wandered from the True Way." Dante's guides,

Virgil and Beatrice, lead him out of the dark forest and direct his journey to the downward spiral of the Inferno, then upward to the height of Mount Purgatory, and then finally to the heavenly realm of Paradise. In other words, the wandering mind, beguiled by the seven deadly vices and the sins of both the body and the mind, easily loses sight of the four last things of death, final judgment, hell, and heaven. The wandering mind no longer grasps the nature of things or comprehends the destiny of man. In his travel through the concentric circles of heaven, Dante notices the phenomenal speed of his progress compared to the plodding movements in hell and the laborious efforts of climbing the mountain of Purgatory: "But how come I to fly / Through these light spheres?" When he asks Beatrice to explain this sudden acceleration, she remarks that his speed should no more astonish him than the movement of water downhill: "You should not, as I see it, marvel more/ At your ascent than at a river's fall/ from a high mountain to the valley floor" (I.i.136-138). To cure the wandering mind of its aberrations, the intelligence must recover this metaphysical truth: everything created possesses a God-given, inborn nature and moves according to the end or destination ascribed to it by the Creator. This nature is fixed and determined forever. Just as planets move in circles, dogs chase rabbits, fire ascends, and water flows downward, man by nature seeks truth and desires God. Happiness follows from man's being true to his nature—to know, love, and serve God in this world and to enjoy eternal happiness in Paradise.

The wandering mind meanders in mazes because it loses sight of the nature of things—the nature of reason, the nature of man, the nature of Fortune, and the nature of God. From his travels, Dante learns that sin deforms man's nature and reduces him to an animal. When he encounters the heretics in the sixth circle of the Inferno, Dante sees sinners in the marsh reduced to frightened frogs: "As frogs before the snake that hunts them down/ churn up their pond in flight, until the last squats on the bottom as if turned to stone-/ so I saw more than a thousand ruined souls/ scatter away from one who crossed dry-shod/ the Stygian marsh into Hell's burning bowels" (IX, 73-78). In the eleventh circle Dante again witnesses a scene that impresses upon him the ugliness of evil. The malicious, the violent, and the fraudulent "lie in the swamp's bowels, those the wind blows about, those the rain beats, and those who meet and clash with such mad howls"—another sight that graphically portrays the effects of sin upon man's nature. In another words, wandering is not harmless travel. To leave home or to depart from the truth inevitably leads to dangers and temptations that lure man to his destruction. Odysseus in his wanderings was subjected to many temptations like the Sirens, Circe, and the Lotus Eaters who offered the pleasures of the senses and the flesh as the ultimate source of happiness. Through Purgatory Dante sees the harm inflicted by the seven deadly sins that reduce man's nature from a noble image of God who stands erect to contemplate God to a lowly creature groveling in the dirt (the punishment for avarice) or creeping slowly bent with a load of heavy stones (the punishment of pride)—a deformation that shocks Dante: " 'Master,' I faltered, that which creeps so slow/ This way—it does not look to me like men;/ It's like—my sight's at fault—I just don't know" (X, 112-114). The danger of wandering, then, is losing one's way to God, being seduced by the snares of the world whether it is the voices of the Sirens or Circe or the glamour of money, pleasure, and power. Wandering follows from being blinded by the false appearance of things and following a road that is not ordered to man's natural destiny of true happiness.

As these examples from literature illustrate, wandering is a universal problem that inflicts misery upon human beings who lose their sense of identity, purpose, and dignity when meandering into the forest or into the maze of human opinions. Modern man also is a notorious wanderer with no guides to return him to the true path. Instead of studying the eternal stars like a wise seaman to find clear direction, modern man ventures further and further into the unknown, the dangerous, and the forbidden with no second thoughts or reservations. As C. S. Lewis observed in *The Great Divorce*, the lost traveler does not find the true way if he travels on the wrong road and continues to move in one direction or another hoping to find his way home. He must return to the place where he first made the wrong turn:

> I do not think that all who choose the wrong road perish; but their rescue consists in being put back on the right road. A wrong sum can be put right: but only by going back till you find the error and working it afresh from that point, never by simply *going on*. Evil can be undone, but it cannot "develop" into good. Time does not heal it.

Once the sexual revolution of the late 1960's unleashed the contraceptive mentality, legalized abortion, no-fault divorce, same-sex marriage, and euthanasia, the Christian moral code of Western civilization lost its authority as a source of eternal truth. Modern man suffered moral homelessness. Without a moral center or "home," the mind wandered into treacherous areas known as reproductive rights, moral relativism, multiculturalism, and radical views of the family and of marriage that have led to unparalleled problems on a scale unprecedented in recent history.

These distortions from the normative moral experience of the human race have transformed Western civilization into the unnatural shapes and grisly sights of Dante's Inferno with all its macabre scenes and punishments. The images of aborted babies and the actual procedure of partial-birth abortion that sucks out the pre-born child's brain after it is punctured with a scissors is as horrific as any scene in Dante's *Inferno*. When the mind wanders from the natural law, the accumulated wisdom of centuries, and the unchanging moral teachings of the Catholic Church, it strays into treacherous waters that destroy civilization. In "The First Vocation Crisis" Jeff Ziegler in *The Catholic World Report* (January 2010) cites the following data that prove the disastrous effects of letting the mind deviate from its true course: a 49 percent decline in marriage from 1970 to 2007; a drop in the birthrate from 3.7 in 1960 to 1.8 in 1980; 39 percent of all births coming from unmarried women; a rise in cohabitation from 439,0000 in 1960 to 6,445,000 in 2007. If one adds to these statistics the over 50 million abortions in the United States alone and the dramatic increase in sexually transmitted diseases, the moral landscape of modern America resembles even more the repulsive terrain of the swamps and marshes of the Inferno with their vile stench.

As Homer, Augustine, Boethius, and Dante demonstrate, the only way out of this morass is to change course and turn homeward, not continue "going on" as C. S. Lewis says on a road that leads to misery, suffering, destruction, disease, and barbarism, a path that can never evolve into good or be healed by time no matter how varied the wanderings or how endless the changes. This continuous reckless wandering from the eternal and natural moral law written on the human heart and enshrined in the Church brings in its wake other immoral monsters that populate the landscape of a modernized Inferno: selective abortions, cloning, in vitro fertilization, embryonic stem-cell research, and medical practices specialized in killing and exploiting human life. God is one, and there is only *one* road that leads upward to the source of truth and wisdom. Evil, however, is legion, and wandering has infinite turns, twists, and windings that lead inevitably to the multiplication of opinions, heresies, and errors that always lead man further away from his true beginning and from his natural destination and from his human and eternal happiness.

Chapter 14. The Empty Self
versus the Rich Soul

On any given weekend many individuals will enter a video store and take home for the weekend, not one classic movie, but five or six videos of mediocre to vulgar quality. On any typical school day a large percentage of children will receive their daily dosage of Ritalin. On any weekday night many families will pass hours being diverted by television or spending hours on the Internet, and on the weekend sports events after sports events will occupy Saturday, Sunday, and Monday night. Estimates of the Couple to Couple League indicate that over eighty percent of childbearing married couples will purchase their supplies of contraceptives and pills as a staple of modern life. These simple observations and indisputable facts reflect an emotional, spiritual, and intellectual starvation which finds relief, not in real nourishment, but in the junk food of modern civilization—the *ersatz* instead of the real. Hollywood's movies imagine themselves as great art, information highways are touted as the equivalent of education, the news media and television assume an aura of reality, and professional sports pose as noble heroism. Despite these attempts to gratify man's interior life with pleasure, peace, entertainment, knowledge, and excitement, man has an inner life that these substitutes for the real thing do not satisfy.

In *The City of God* Augustine explains the hierarchy of Being in the order of nature. Of the beings which exist those which have life (plants) rank above those which have none (rocks); among living things "the sentient are higher than those which have no sensation, as animals are ranked above trees." Among the sentient, humans endowed with intelligence occupy a higher place than animals, and above mortal humans are the pure spirits, the immortal angels. In this order of nature only God, angels, and humans experience an inner life. While rocks have being, plants reproduce, and animals experience pleasure and pain, only God, angels, and men possess a rational and spiritual nature endowed with the power to know, love, and choose. This inner life, which John Donne in *Devotions* describes as "a little world," is the intellectual, emotional, and moral realm in which humans discern the true, the beautiful, and the good:

> It is too little to call man a little world; except God, man is diminutive to nothing. Man consists of more pieces, more parts, than the world; than the world doth, nay, than the world is. And if those pieces were extended, and stretched out in man as they are in the world, man would be the giant, and the world the dwarf; the world but the map, and the man the world. (Meditation IV)

Indeed this inner world is a universe of profound depths that encompasses a vast range of thoughts, sensitivities, and perceptions. St. Thomas Aquinas writes that man is *capax universi*, capable of understanding the whole of reality. Humans philosophize about all of reality from the origin of life to the end of human existence, and they contemplate all the mysteries and miracles of creation from the glory of the stars to the wonder of love. Humans experience a full range of emotion—the tenderness of adoring a baby, the affection between parents and children, the bonds of close friendship, the ecstasy of *eros*, and the communion between God and man. Humans sense beauty in all its myriad expressions from the human form and nature's glory to music, painting, dance, poetry, and architecture. The inner life encompasses a whole spectrum of feelings: the laughter of children, the passion of lovers, the devotion of spouses, the loyalty of friends, the patriotism of soldiers, and the love of saints. The range of the inner life spans a wide distance from the lightheartedness of mirth to the sorrow of tragedy to the peace that passes all understanding. Thus the inner life is a world or universe copiously rich and full, *capax universi*, capable of loving and knowing and designed to grasp the transcendentals of truth, goodness, and beauty. Again, as Donne writes in *Devotions*, "Our creatures are our thoughts, creatures that are born giants; that reach from east to west, from earth to heaven; that do not only bestride all the sea and land, but span the sun and firmament at once; my thoughts reach all, comprehend all" (Meditation IV).

Just as the body requires nourishment to gratify the hunger of the appetite and achieve the rest that accompanies repletion, the soul also demands satisfaction in its need for completeness. The interior life is intended for fullness and wholeness, for as Christ said, "I am come that they might have life, and that they might have it more abundantly" (John 10: 10). The inner life requires the food of joy, love, truth, goodness, beauty, and God to experience the depths of happiness in the soul and the heart. A bona fide moral education in the home and a real intellectual cultivation in schools enrich the resources of the inner life and deepen the sense of this capacious "world." Teaching the young the riches and traditions of the Christian faith develops the interior life of prayer, reflection, and contemplation and lifts the mind and heart to the reality of God. The purpose of civilization and culture is the transmission of ideals that enhance the inner life and inspire the soul to seek the things that are above. The sacrament of marriage, like all the sacraments, deepens this interior life by penetrating the mystery of the heart's profound desire to give and to receive. A human life, then, requires a constant filling and receiving of the wholesome, life-giving food for the mind, heart, and soul that refreshes the entire being of the person and reaches the depths of the heart. Families, schools, societies, churches, and culture all play vital roles in the formation or deformation of this inner life.

Because nature abhors a vacuum, the inner life does not remain a void. Deprived of natural joy, human love, universal truths, divine wisdom, and transcendent beauty, the soul, heart, and mind seek substitutes for reality and fill the emptiness with alternatives that lack substance. Absent the blessings of family life, the joys of marriage, the classic expressions of truth and beauty, the riches of the *philosophia perennis*, the wisdom of the past, and the eternal verities of religion, the inner life atrophies and seeks satisfaction through imitations of the real thing. Obsessive, compulsive habits of eating, drinking, and spending replace a normal life of simplicity, frugality, and moderation. Mindless entertainment, restless consumerism, inane video culture, and sports mania detract from the time spent in the human interaction of conversation, friendship, and hospitality. The interior world, then, becomes a wasteland, and the happiness of a rich inner life deteriorates into the boredom of the empty self—a life in which man can only "measure out my life with coffee spoons" and "spit out all the butt-ends of my days and ways" as T.S. Eliot writes in "The Love Song of J. Alfred Prufrock."

In Book IV of *Gulliver's Travels* Swift satirizes a presumably utopian society of horses, the Houyhnhnms, because they are devoid of an inner life. While the horses imagine themselves to live in a utopia because of their superior health and the absence of social evils like alcoholism, war, and venereal disease in their country, they have no family life. They show no special tenderness or fond affection for their own children: they exchange their offspring with other families so that a balance of equal numbers of male and female prevails in each household. Exercising rational control of their passions and appetites at all times, the Houyhnhnms congratulate themselves for resisting the deadly sins of gluttony, avarice, lust, and wrath. However, the horses have no life of the mind or soul. They do not wonder at beauty or goodness, they do not contemplate God or eternity, and they do not delight in music, sports, poetry, or art. Practicing benevolence and humanitarianism, the Houyhnhnms love their whole race and exchange goods with one another; no member of their society is deprived of the basic necessities of life: "They will have it that *Nature* teaches them to love the whole Species." Nevertheless, even though the horses give the impression of living contented, fulfilled lives, their existence is drab and monotonous. They have no aesthetic sense, no spiritual life, and no intellectual pursuits. They do not laugh or cry, experience neither love nor sorrow, and have no desire to enlarge their minds or broaden their worlds. Emotionally stunted and intellectually undeveloped, the Houyhnhnms simply survive, but they do not live abundant, rich lives and show no sense of a mind *capax universi*. Despite their physical health, peaceful society, and distribution of goods, they live an empty existence.

Without joy, love, goodness, beauty, truth, and God the inner life dies as Huxley's *Brave New World* verifies. No normal, human interior life is possible with the destruction of the family. In *Brave New World* the family is obsolete because children are conceived in test tubes in assembly-line production in the Central London Hatchery and Conditioning Centre. The young are reared in government-controlled nurseries where they are conditioned for their social destiny as determined by the Controllers of the state. Love and life are separated, and sexuality and procreation are divorced. The motto of the day is "civilization is sterilization," and the words "mother" and "father" are words of reproach: "To say one was a mother—that was past a joke; it was an obscenity." Natural childbirth rather than test-tube conception in a modern fertilizing room carries with it a stigma, the pejorative phrase "gross viviparous reproduction," and fatherhood is equally disgusting: "The word for 'father' was not so much obscene as . . . merely gross, a scatological rather than pornographic impropriety." As incubators and test tubes replace mothers and fathers and nurseries assume the role of families, the emptiness of the inner life requires the cult of pleasure to fill the void. The drug "soma" ("Euphoric, narcotic, pleasantly hallucinant"), the Feelies (pornographic movies), and sexual license ("everyone belongs to everyone else") fill the vacuum. The junk food of modern culture replaces the real nourishment for human beings.

The inner life also requires beauty and truth for its fulfillment, but these transcendentals have been replaced by convenience and ease in *Brave New World*. Mustapha Mond, the controller of this utopian society, explains that a brave new world demands censorship to eliminate the influence of the wisdom and art of the past upon the present and to prevent a critical comparison between the way things are and the way things ought to be: "We haven't any use for old things here. . . . Particularly when they're beautiful. Beauty's attractive, and we don't want people to be attracted by old things. We want them to like the new ones." Thus Shakespeare's plays, the Holy Bible, *The Imitation of Christ*, and the works of Cardinal Newman are all notably absent from the schools, libraries, and society of the new world. The ideological revolution in *Brave New World*, according to the controller, has been "to shift the emphasis from truth and beauty to comfort and happiness." Whereas "knowledge was the highest good, truth the supreme value" in ages past, utility, efficiency, ease, and instant gratification are the *summum bonum* in the utopia of the modern world. The empty self devoid of beauty and truth requires constant external stimulation, sensationalistic entertainment, and an endless supply of drugs and pills. To minister to the emptiness of the interior life, Lenina, typical of the women in her society, "wore a silver mounted green morocco-surrogate cartridge belt, bulging with the regulation supply of contraceptives." Drugs and pills substitute for truth and beauty. Hence, instead of truth, beauty, love, or God as the nourishment of the inner life and the food of the soul, human happiness is redefined as "seven and a half hours of mild, unexhausting labor, and then the soma ration and games and unrestricted copulation and the feelies."

The empty self knows neither the ecstasy of love and joy nor the agony of tragedy and death, and it reflects no sense of mystery, wonder, or contemplation. It does not experience moments that illuminate the heart of reality like the scene at the garden of Ostia in Augustine's *Confessions* where he describes the depths of the inner life of the soul. Augustine and his mother Monica experienced the palpable presence and nearness of God at the garden of Ostia after Augustine's conversion—an answer to his mother's prayers:

> . . . we proceeded step by step through all bodily things up to that heaven whence shine the sun and the moon and the stars down upon the earth. We ascended higher yet by means of inward thought and discourse and admiration of your works, and we came up to our own minds. We transcended them, so that we attained to the region of abundance that never fails, in which you feed Israel forever upon the food of truth, and where life is that Wisdom by which all these things are made, both which have been and which are to be. (Book IX)

At this moment Augustine and Monica discern the Divine Providence of God in their lives and the personal, tender, sensitive love of God for each of them: "Thou lovest us, Lord, as if we were the only one." They encounter the mystery of a God "most hidden and most present, most beautiful and most strong, stable and incomprehensible." Monica's and Augustine's hearts are melted by God's love, and they are in awe at the hand of God in the plan of their lives: "Your love pierced our heart like an arrow, and we bore within us your words, transfixing our inmost parts." Experiencing the depths of human and divine love, Augustine and Monica experience a peace that the world cannot give and encounter a foretaste of Heaven on earth: . . ."we proceeded step by step up through all bodily things up to that heaven whence shine the sun and the moon and the stars down upon the earth."

Jaded and blasé, the empty self lacks passion and depth. Like the cold, insensible Houyhnhnms and the dehumanized, deadened inhabitants of Brave New World, the empty self—unlike the Psalmist—never cries, sings, praises, gives thanks, or wonders. No powerful pleas for mercy like "Out of the depths have I cried unto thee, O Lord" (Psalm 130) or pangs of longing like "As the hart panteth after the water brooks, so panteth my soul after thee, O God .My soul thirsteth for God, for the living God" (Psalm 42) inspire the empty self. No rapturous transports of love—like Romeo's wonder at the miracle of love and awe at Juliet's beauty—move the hearts of the impoverished soul:

> O, she doth teach the torches to burn bright!
> It seems she hangs upon the cheek of night
> As a rich jewel in an Ethiop's ear—
> Beauty too rich for use, for earth too dear.
> (I. v. 45-48)

The empty self does not know the thrill of beauty which Gerard Manley Hopkins captures in famous lines like

"Glory be to God for dappled things-/ For skies of couple-colour as a brinded cow" or "The world is charged with the grandeur of God. / It will flame out, like shining from shook foil." The empty self does not know the dark night of the soul or the valley of the shadow of death that John Donne plumbs in "A Nocturnal Upon St. Lucy's Day, Being the Shortest Day," a poem that depicts the broken heart and inconsolable grief of a husband who laments the loss of his beloved wife:

> For I am every dead thing,
> In whom Love wrought new alchemy;
> For his art did express
> A quintessence even from nothingness,
> From dull privations and lean emptiness.
> He ruined me, and I am rebegot
> Of absence, darkness, death: things which
> are not.

Thus neither love nor death, neither goodness nor beauty, and neither sin nor guilt stir the heart or move the soul of the empty self. No one in the society of the Houyhnhnms or in Huxley's Brave New World speaks in the impassioned eloquence of a King Lear outraged by the enormity of the evil he has suffered:

> Blow, winds, and crack your cheeks! Rage, blow!
> You cataracts and hurricanoes, spout
> Till you have drenched our steeples, drowned
> the cocks!
> You sulphurous and thought-executing fires,
> Vaunt-couriers to oak-cleaving thunderbolts,

Singe my white head! And thou, all-shaking
thunder,
Strike flat the thick rotundity o' the world!
Crack nature's molds, all germains spill at
once,
That make ingrateful man! (III.ii. 1-9)

In all these examples from Augustine to King Lear,
the heart is full, the soul is moved, the conscience is
awakened, and the mind is alive The agony of suffering
and the ecstasy of joy are felt profoundly, and the
sentiments pour forth from the riches of the interior
life that overflows with song, tears, wonder, gratitude,
or love.

Why is the empty self devoid of these emotions?
What, then, separates the empty self from the full
interior world? Nothing can come from nothing. If
the heart is not formed, cold, insensitive beings like
the Houyhnhmns result. If the family is deconstructed,
the people of a Brave New World hatch human beings
conditioned to eschew fatherhood and motherhood
as "obscene" and "gross". If the ideals of purity and
fruitful, faithful married love do not govern a society,
then the motto of "civilization is sterilization" in *Brave
New World* leads to a death wish—a contraceptive
mentality where populations refuse to replace themselves.
If education is reduced to political ideology and moral
relativism, the mind never acquires a taste for the love of
truth or savors the goodness of wisdom. If a person lives
on a constant intellectual, spiritual, and emotional diet
lacking substance, the emptiness is never filled. The heart,
mind, and soul atrophy without proper nourishment,
and leave a void. The junk food that fills this vacuum

never gives rest, peace or fulfillment. As Socrates explains in the *Gorgias*, the confectioner pampers the body with sweets whereas the physician knows the difference between nutritious and unhealthy foods: "Thus cookery puts on the mask of medicine and pretends to know what foods are best for the body, and, if an audience of children had to decide whether a confectioner or a doctor is the better judge of wholesome and unwholesome foodstuffs, the doctor would unquestionably die of hunger." The confectioner, Socrates explains, is a caterer who "panders" to intemperate desires that are never gratified, resembling a leaky cask or sieve that empties as soon as filled. The empty self resembles the man whom Socrates describes as constantly itching: "Can a man who itches and wants to scratch and whose opportunities of scratching are unbounded be said to lead a happy life continually scratching?"

Whereas the empty self is constantly itching, the rich soul is replete with energy and substance. Consumer of beer, cigarettes, contraceptives, pills, professional sports, entertainment, news, and television, the empty self feeds itself on nothing. Addicted to titillation, violence, sensationalism, and sloth, the empty self gorges itself on the confectioners' sugar that does not satisfy the hunger of the soul. The souls of fools, Socrates argues, resemble sieves because "they are leaky and unable to retain their contents." The rich soul, however, knows the real thing from its imitation, the substantive from the ephemeral, and the transitory from the eternal. Romeo's love for Juliet is the real thing, the powerful attraction of a passionate man for a beautiful woman whom he longs to marry—not the mechanical, impersonal, contraceptive lovemaking of the couples in *Brave New World*.

Monica's maternal love is the real thing, a mother's heart praying longingly day and night for her wayward son's conversion—not some cant about motherhood as absurd and "gross". Hopkins' sense of beauty is the real thing, a sense of awe and wonder at the inexhaustible, copious nature of beauty in all the colorfulness and variety of nature's combinations from "Rose moles all in stipple upon trout that swim" to "Landscape plotted and pieced-fold, fallow, and plough." As Hopkins writes in another poem, "For Christ plays in ten thousand places." Nothing is truly beautiful that does not reflect God. David's longing for God ("As the hart panteth after the water brooks") is the real thing—not the need for more soma, more pills, more drugs or more Ritalin. Donne's dark night of the soul as he passes through the valley of the shadow of death is the real thing, the agony of losing a loved one—not some stoical apathy to human loss or some cold rationalization about the naturalness of death and dying. King Lear's righteous anger over his "serpent-like" and "pelican" daughters' cruel ingratitude is the real thing, honest passion at the enormity of life's injustice—not passive tolerance of or acquiescent indifference to the ugliness of evil.

Instead of the real thing, the empty self gluts itself on husks. "Safe sex" pretends to be love, cohabitation poses as marriage, and same-sex unions ape matrimony, but they do not penetrate the transcendent mystery of love or the sacramental nature of marriage as total giving that Romeo and Juliet experience: "My bounty is as boundless as the sea, / My love as deep; the more I give to thee, / The more I have, for both are infinite." Feminism claims to restore women's rights and to elevate her power, but it does not glimpse the maternal heart of true femininity that Monica's genius exemplifies. In Augustine's words to God, "Could you refuse your help to her or despise her tears with which she asked from you, not gold or silver or any mutable and transitory good, but the salvation of her son's soul? . . . No, you could not." In the world of advertising and in the mass media, image, fashion, and glamour disguise themselves as the quintessence of the beautiful, but they never detect the secret of true beauty that Hopkins' poetry seizes: all human natural beauty—spiritual in origin—reflects the glory of God: "I know the beauty of the Lord by it," Hopkins remarked about the bluebell. In a culture of death where abortion and euthanasia in their commonplaceness desensitize consciences and harden hearts, Donne exposes the hard truth: death is absolute evil and a product of hell, "the grave of all that's nothing"—total negation, deprivation, and absence, "things which are not." In the politically correct world where non-judgmental tolerance is the ultimate proof of goodness and moral outrage is the capital sin, King Lear demonstrates honest realism as he erupts with thunderous anger at the unnatural depravity of "the marble-hearted" ingratitude of daughters to whom he "gave all" and received nothing. Whereas the ideology of moral relativism feigns neutrality about right and wrong on the basis of diversity, Lear is repelled by the horror of evil and does not equivocate: "Ingratitude, thou marble-hearted fiend, / More hideous when thou show'st thee in a child/ Than the sea monster" (I. iv. 256-258). While the empty selves of the Houyhnhnms and the citizens of the Brave New World act smugly complacent in their imaginary paradise devoid of God, the Psalmist attributes all true happiness to the reality of God's Providence: "Bless the Lord, O my soul, and all that is within me, bless his holy name" and "O give thanks to the Lord, for he is good." Thus the real food of the soul—truth—nourishes the interior world and enriches it with abundant life—a copiousness that overflows into moral sentiments, refined feelings, and passionate hearts that distinguish human beings as the image of God. The rich soul reflects a whole universe, the entire range of human thought and feeling, and can repeat, with Edmund Burke in *Reflections on the Revolution in France*, "We preserve the whole of our feelings still native and entire, unsophisticated by pedantry and infidelity. We have real hearts of flesh and blood beating in our bosoms."

The empty self, on the other hand, is a stunted soul. "Real hearts of flesh and blood" are not in evidence. The Houyhnhnms do not mourn their dead, and the inhabitants of Brave New World reduce death to "an eternal soma holiday": . . . "as though death were something terrible, as though anyone mattered as much as all that," remarks the nurse in Huxley's novel. Empty souls feel no shock, disgust, or horror at abortion, partial-birth abortion (infanticide) or physician-assisted suicide. The Houyhnhnms barter and exchange their children, and the citizens of Brave New World reproduce themselves in the test tubes and incubators of the fertilizing room of the Central London Hatchery and Conditioning Centre. Empty souls engage in the grisly business of fetal harvesting, buying, selling, and experimenting on the bodies of aborted babies. Human cloning is the standard procedure in Brave New World: "Millions of identical twins. The principle of mass production at last applied to biology." Empty souls react with diabolical blandness to the news that Advanced Cell Technology in Massachusetts has successfully cloned human embryos for "harvesting" cells—creating life to destroy life. Living the primitive life of noble savages, the Houyhnhnms do not enlarge their minds but remain ignorant of great art, music, poetry, and architecture. Education in *Brave New World* likewise deprives pupils of "the best that has been thought and said" (Matthew Arnold's famous phrase), for the Controller argues, "We haven't any use for old things here" and adds "Particularly when they're beautiful." Empty souls label Western civilization "Eurocentric," revile the classics as the work of "dead white men," and invoke the dogma of multiculturalism as a higher knowledge surpassing the wisdom of the ages. Instead of real hearts of flesh and blood that recognize the difference between good and evil, that know when to cry, rejoice, wonder, or give thanks like David in the Psalms, empty souls resemble creatures that C.S. Lewis called "men without chests"— men without magnanimity, chivalry, nobility, honor, principles, or conscience. Men without chests are half-alive, dehumanized, insensitive, and heartless. In Lewis's words, "It is not excess of thought but defect of fertile and generous emotion that marks them out." The empty souls lack "the spirited element" that Plato speaks of in *The Republic.* Their interior life is not, in Donne's phrase, "a little world" in touch with the divine life of the larger universe—the realities of truth, love, goodness, and beauty—but "the wasteland" that characterizes the modern soul in T. S. Eliot's poetry. The menu of life offers other choices besides the expensive, addictive, advertised junk food of the mind that promises much but offers nothing. The bill of fare also features the food of the gods, the riches of milk and honey, and the gifts of nectar and ambrosia—the natural, God-given cornucopia of family, religion, wisdom, art, love, beauty, and joy that are the real thing. As Savage, the visitor to Brave New World who is disgusted by the dehumanized lives of the empty souls, protests: "But I don't want comfort. I want God, I want poetry, I want real danger, I want freedom, I want goodness, I want sin."

Chapter 15. The Inspiration of the Muses and the Power of Beauty

The ancient Greeks bequeathed to Western civilization the notion of the Muses, the nine goddesses of inspiration who preside over music, dance, poetry, and drama that enrich ordinary life with the delights of beauty and wonder evoked by great art. Epic poetry, for example, always invokes the Muse to lift the song and story of the poet to the most sublime heights. Thus Homer begins the *Odyssey*, "The hero of the tale which I beg the Muse to help me tell," and Virgil in the *Aeneid,* also seeks divine help: "I pray for inspiration, to tell how it all began. . . ." The Greek ideal of civilization, the art of living *well*, to use Aristotle's phrase, always incorporates the aspects of the beautiful in all its many forms to distinguish a human life from a barbaric existence. In Pericles' famous funeral oration from Thucydides' *The Peloponnesian War,* the Greek statesman defined the Greek way of life as filled with the presence and influence of the Muses: "And we have not forgotten to provide for our weary spirits many relaxations from toil; we have regular games and sacrifices throughout the year; our homes are beautiful and elegant; and the delight which we daily feel in all these things helps to banish melancholy."

Through the *Odyssey* Homer depicts many scenes of hospitality that welcome travelers. The Muses attend these festive banquets as the rites of hospitality provide not only food and shelter to the visitor but also an opportunity for conversation, storytelling, song, and dance. Alcinous, the king of Phaeacia, introduces Demodocus, the favorite bard "whom the Muses loved above all others," to entertain Odysseus with the music of "his heavenly gift of delighting our ears whatever theme he chooses for his song." As the bard plays his lyre, he is soon accompanied by a "band of expert dancers" who move Odysseus to wonder at the exquisite beauty of their art as "their feet came down to the sacred floor with a scintillating movement that filled Odysseus with admiration as he watched." Odysseus calls these experiences of hospitality visited by the Muses "something like perfection"—the supreme moments of life's sweetness.

The Muses, then, provide relief from the drudgery of toil, dispel sadness, and offer relief to the tedium and monotony of life. As Plato writes in *The Laws*, without the Muses and the spirit of play, recreation, and leisure they bring into human life, man lives a dehumanized existence: "But the gods, taking pity on human beings—a race born to labor—gave them regularly recurring divine festivals, as a means of refreshment from their fatigue; they gave them the Muses, and Apollo and Dionysius as the leaders of the Muses, to the end that, after refreshing themselves in the company of the gods, they might return to an upright posture." The burden of work without relief and a life of mere survival without the beauty of the arts and the leisure of celebrations inspired by the Muses reduce man to a brutish existence indistinguishable from the life of animals. The Muses illuminate the classical distinction between the servile arts and liberal arts—the difference between those things man does as a means to an end like earning money and those things that man does as an end in itself like the enjoyment of recreation that is desirable for its pure goodness. The nourishment of the spirit and the life of the soul need the Muses as much as the body requires food and sleep.

The shield of Achilles in the *Iliad* presents many scenes from the daily life of the Greeks: a city at war and a city at peace, the sowing of the fields and the harvest of the land, judges working in a court of law to achieve a wise verdict and wedding guests celebrating with dancing, flutes, and harps as the bride marches. In all these incidents man does not live by bread alone. Play follows work, and the Muses fill the occasions with the spirit of festivity. These pictures show that man requires leisure and the inspiration of the Muses to transcend mere physical existence—to live well and to enjoy the beauty of the arts that allow man to go beyond the struggle for survival. A civilized culture allows time for the enjoyment of life's highest and finest pleasures.

As the harvesters reap the harvest of the grain, the servants and women prepare the feast to renew body and the spirit. As the grape pickers gather the clusters that produce the mellow wine, music fills the air as a boy plays a lyre, and "all the rest followed, all together, frisking, singing, shouting, their dancing footsteps beating out the time." Man not only labors first to enjoy the pleasures of the Muses later but also recognizes that some human experiences are simply intrinsically good and loved for the sheer joy they bring. Some pure joys do not depend on harvesting the grain or picking the grapes but are simply good in and of themselves. In one of the final scenes on the shield, Homer depicts a circle of youths in "fine-spun tunics" and maidens "crowned with a bloom of fresh garlands" who "danced and danced" in rapturous glee. They dance for pure pleasure and the love of the dance itself. The Muses, then, accompany man in his daily rounds of toil in the field and in the home to alleviate the weariness of repetitious work without relief that leads to dehumanization.

In Willa Cather's *My Antonia*, the narrator, Jim Burden, recalls a turning point in his education at the University of Nebraska when his Latin teacher, Gaston Cleric, explained one of the lines from Virgil's *Georgics* that translates "for I shall be the first, if I live, to bring the Muse into my country." The Latin *patria* (fatherland), the professor explained, does not mean "a nation or even a province, but the little rural neighborhood on the Mincio where the poet was born." Cleric lauded Virgil's introduction of the Muses to the Roman people as the poet's greatest accomplishment, even more important than the *Aeneid*, the epic that remained unfinished at his death. Jim remembers his teacher's passionate convictions on the passage, his interpretation that Virgil during his final days "must have said to himself with the thankfulness of a good man, 'I was the first to bring the Muse into my own country.'" In other words, Virgil saw the value of the Muses as the birthright of all human beings, not simply the legacy of a privileged class of the educated, the wealthy patrons of the arts. From Greece Virgil brought the goddesses of inspiration not merely to the capital or to the palaces but to the small farms, villages and "to his father's fields, 'slopping down to the river and to the old beech trees with broken tops'."

Pondering the wisdom of his Latin professor, Jim soon experiences first-hand Virgil's ideal of the presence of the Muses in the smallest towns or most obscure places. On the evening after the class on Virgil, Jim proceeds to study in a half-hearted, lackadaisical way with a weary spirit until an unexpected guest appears. Professor Cleric's words come alive when a visitor knocks at the door. While Jim ruminates if "some particular rocky strip of New England coast about which he had so often told me was Cleric's *patria*," a Muse arrives in the form of the beautiful, vivacious Lena Lingard, a beloved childhood friend from his early life on the prairie who comes like a goddess breathing life into Jim's lonely existence. Jim's mood and the whole atmosphere of the room are infused with the passion, energy, and warmth that Lena brings. He realizes the power of one person to change prosaic dullness into lively poetry: "If there were no girls like them in the world, there would be no poetry."

As Jim learns, Lena recently moved from the farm to Lincoln, Nebraska, to do business as dressmaker in the town where Jim studies at the university. During this enjoyable time of renewed friendship, Jim compliments Lena for her lovely appearance and her elegant style, enjoys her delightful, lighthearted conversation on their happy childhood memories, and receives an invitation to attend the theater with her to rekindle their fond relationship from the past. After Lena says good-night, Jim notices the change in atmosphere in his room and the rejoicing of his spirits; "Lena had left something warm and friendly in the lamplight. How I loved to hear her laugh again!" Lena's friendship, beauty, laughter, and warmth transfigure the plain room and Jim's listless disposition into a place of jubilation and mirth. Her presence reminded him of all the immigrant girls he played with on the farm who made life joy-filled by their kind hearts and joie de vivre. Professor Cleric's lesson on Virgil's love of the Muses profoundly touched Jim in a personal way: "It came over me, as it had done never before, the relation between girls like those and the poetry of Virgil." Lena lifted Jim's spirits in the way the Muses breathe life into the heart and soul.

Human beings, then, like the nine Muses, infuse inspiration that changes the monotonous quality of life and overcomes the apathy that afflicts the human spirit. From Homer to Plato to Virgil to Willa Cather this wisdom about the necessity of leisure, play, beauty, friendship, music, and dance keeps life human, balanced, and whole. *My Antonia* especially illuminates the importance of persons as sources of inspiration who touch hearts and lift spirits. Whenever Jim remembers Antonia in her childhood, he recalls her vibrant, radiant nature, especially her fun-loving exuberance and robust vitality: always showing gladness when seeing Jim as she laughs and squeezes his hand; racing across the prairie to visit him for her reading lesson and reveling in their friendship; and running with Jim to explore the wildlife on the prairie with "eyes big and warm and full of light." Jim remembers Antonia's love of family, her fondness for playing with children, and her gracious, hospitable nature that always greeted others with spontaneous affection and invitations as when she accidentally sees Jim and insists that he join her and the other Bohemian girls on a picnic.

To Jim Burden, Antonia and the immigrant girls possessed "a kind of hearty joviality, a relish of life, not overdelicate, but very invigorating"—an embrace of life's joys and goodness that they expressed in their honest feelings, beautiful appearance, love of dancing, and fun-loving natures. Jim appreciated Antonia's heartfelt sincerity, display of warm emotions, and truthful words: "Everything she said came right out of her heart."

Jim always noticed in Antonia a natural, uninhibited freedom of movement that she especially exhibited in dancing. Unlike the conventional, prim, American girls of the merchants who avoided domestic work, Antonia and Lena excelled as cooks and housekeepers and were never embarrassed about being hired help to assist their parents earn a livelihood. They put their heart and soul into all their work. Jim noticed that the refined American girls were not graceful dancers or interesting conversationalists ("their bodies never moved inside their clothes; their muscles seemed to ask but one thing—not to be disturbed"), whereas Antonia had "so much spring and variety, and was always putting in new steps and slides." Like Lena, Antonia was one of the Muses who brought poetry into Jim's life.

After a separation of twenty years as Jim and Antonia settle into their adult lives and now live in different states, Jim finds an opportunity to pay Antonia a visit as he travels by railroad from the West coast to New England. Even after twenty years of ageing, managing a farm with her husband, and caring for ten children, Antonia impresses Jim as a woman whose "inner glow" had not faded: "Whatever else was gone, Antonia had not lost the fire of her life." Her many children, "a veritable explosion of life," find their mother a storehouse of delight as Jim did in his childhood as they turn to her for stories and fun. Seeing Antonia in middle-age after the passage of many years, Jim sees on a larger scale than ever that "She was a rich mine of life, like the founders of early races"—abundant in the generous giving of herself in all the expressions of love.

Life without the Muses or without the poetry of beautiful, vivacious women with generous hearts and loving ways soon degenerates into the drabness and dinginess of threadbare lives in which man lives only to work and survive, never seeing the stars, never wondering at the splendor of the world, never learning to dance, sing, play, or love, and never appreciating the riches and depths of goodness in other human beings. Recalling their special friendship in the course of an entire lifetime, Jim fondly says, "You really are a part of me." Antonia replies, "Ain't it wonderful, Jim, how much people can mean to each other? I'm so glad we had each other when we were little." The Muses make a difference in the culture of a society just as Lena, Antonia, and Jim enriched and added to each other's lives.

Other characters in literature infuse the energy of the Muses and the poetry of the art of living into the humdrum existence of others. In *At the Back of the North Wind* the young boy Diamond enlivens the household by his playful imagination that fills the air with mirth when he invents nursery rhymes for baby brother. The baby bursts with laughter when he hears such music as "baby baby babbing/your father's gone a-cabbing/to catch a shilling for its pence/ to make the baby babbing dance." When the mother reads nursery rhymes to Diamond like "I know a river/ whose waters run asleep/ run run run/ singing in the shallows/ dumb in the hollows/ or in the shallows/ sleeping so deep/ and all the swallows . . .," Diamond guesses that the author must have lived "at the back of the North Wind," that is, some divine world where angels and fairies revel in childlike glee and pure happiness that overflows into their spirits and into the lives of all they touch to dispel melancholy, desperation, and fear.

Even though Diamond's father suffers an injury that prevents him from earning his livelihood and his worried mother is filled with anxiety about the future, Diamond changes the somber mood of the home. The mother complains, "It's a sad world!" And Diamond responds, "Is it? I don't know." The mother grieves at the thought of shortage of food without her husband's income, but Diamond answers, "But the birds get through the winter, don't they?" When Diamond suggests that they borrow food from an aunt, that he can earn money to provide for the family, and that father will find eventually work, the mother asks, "How do you know that?" The child answers, "I don't know it. But I haven't even a cupboard, and I've always had plenty to eat." He adds, "I think there must be a big cupboard somewhere, out of which the little cupboards are filled, you know, mother." To be at the back of the North Wind means to feel the power of divine inspirations and to experience glimpses of heavenly bliss that fill the heart with great ebullient joy that spreads to others.

Boswell's *Life of Johnson* also depicts a man of robust energy, lively conversation, and affectionate friendship who fills a room with wit, wisdom, and cheer. A man of passionate temperament renowned for his "intellectual vigour" and "ardent love of literature," Dr. Johnson enlivened company with his convivial spirit and "clubbable" British affability. Boswell observed that Johnson "had no shyness, real or affected, but was easy of access to all who were properly recommended." He praises the eminent man of letters for the stimulation he always provided: "But his conversation was so rich, so animated, and so forcible. . . ." The famous actor David Garrick also relished Johnson's refreshing, spirited companionship: "He is the first man in the world for sprightly conversation."

Johnson especially displayed his lively mind when presented with nonsensical ideas and pretentious attitudes he ridiculed as "cant." When Boswell cited the boasts of two of their acquaintances, David Hume and Samuel Foote, testifying to their fearlessness of death, Johnson retorts, "He may tell you, he holds his finger in the flame of a candle, without feeling pain; would you believe him? . . . Hold a pistol to Foote's breast, or to Hume's breast, and threaten to kill them, and you'll see how they behave." Johnson's company was welcomed, savored, and valued by all in his circle of friendship. After his death one beloved friend paid him this memorable tribute: "He has made a chasm, which not only nothing can fill up, but which nothing has a tendency to fill up. Johnson is dead. Let us go to the next best:—there is no body; no man can be said to put you in mind of Johnson."

Exerting the influence of a Muse, Johnson breathed life. Always revitalizing his old friendships and welcoming new acquaintances, he cultivated these relationships by weekly visits and frequent correspondence—a habit he explained in famous words of wisdom: "A man, Sir, should keep his friendship *in constant repair*." Johnson's friendship brought affection, mirth, and kindness to dear friends, especially to Anna Williams, a blind widow for whom Johnson provided lodgings. His conversation energized intellectual life and made the exchange of ideas an exhilarating experience as seen in the famous Literary Club that met regularly at the Turk's Head Inn for dinner, conversation, and fellowship. Johnson's example and inspiration also changed lives.

Known for his integrity and scrupulous adherence to truthfulness in words and facts, Johnson's friends prone to exaggeration, caricature, and intemperate language, always measured their words in his company. Boswell observes, "He inculcated upon all his friends the importance of perpetual vigilance against the slightest degree of falsehood; the effect of which, as Sir Joshua Reynolds observed . . . has been, that all who were of his *school* are distinguished for a love of truth and accuracy. . . ."

The Muses acknowledge man's need for art, beauty, play, and leisure to live well. Some things are to be loved and enjoyed for their own sake, not for any utilitarian reason. Man's soul and heart need the emotional nourishment that inspiration provides to give life to the spirit. Daily life and ordinary work do not have to reduce man to a drab, dreary existence unrelieved by the fruits of leisure. Work without play dehumanizes man and does not allow for the transcendence, contemplation, and wonder that the Muses bring. Life without the poetry of women like Antonia and Lena filling it with their love of life, delight in beauty, and enjoyment of people reduces man's lot to mere endurance or survival. A life without people like Lena, Antonia, Diamond, and Dr. Johnson to teach us how to laugh, dance, play, wonder, love, converse, tell stories, and live abundant lives is dead and lifeless—an impoverished existence resembling an Orwellian universe notorious for its bland, tepid, colorless quality that Winston Smith describes so well in *1984*: "It struck him that the truly characteristic thing about modern life was not its cruelty or insecurity, but simply its bareness, its dinginess, its listlessness."

Chapter 16. The Art of Seeing: Discovering the Truth, Looking at the Whole, and Glimpsing the Center

The English language contains many words for the various acts of seeing, for example, staring, gaping, scrutinizing, ogling, glancing, beholding, and contemplating. The eye, the most cognitive of the five senses, allows for a comprehensive vision of the world—the ability to look above at the stars, to see vistas and prospects from mountains, to exercise a peripheral vision that extends from left to right and from up to down, and to admire works of art in the intricacy of their design. Nevertheless, having eyes does not mean that a person always sees, sees vital distinctions, or sees the fullness of the truth. True seeing is the art of discovering what is truly there, looking at the whole, discerning differences, and glimpsing the center. A person's sight may see the whole but overlook the part, notice details but miss the larger picture, look at the superficial but overlook the essential, or observe only the visible things without recognizing that, in St. Paul's words, the invisible things of God are known by the visible. Many classic works of literature illuminate this distinction between those who have eyes and see and those who see not.

In Robert Frost's "The Star-Splitter" Brad McLaughlin, an apathetic farmer with an avocation for astronomy, often tells the neighbors he plans to sell his farm, spend the money on a telescope, and devote more time to his favorite pastime of star-gazing. However, instead of selling his meager farm, one day he sets fire to his home to collect the fire insurance and purchase the expensive telescope he equates with great learning and true happiness. He rationalizes his decision by telling his neighbors, "I'll have one if I sell my farm to buy it" and justifies his extravagant expense with the argument that "the best thing that we're put here for's to see;/ The strongest thing that's given us to see with's/ A telescope." Buying a $600 telescope and abandoning farming, the "hugger-mugger" farmer imagines he has elevated himself from the humble work of tilling the land to the wondrous raptures of seeing the stars. The telescope, named the Star-Splitter "Because it didn't do a thing but split/ A star in two or three, the way you split/A globule of quicksilver in your hand," performs its function, but the study of astronomy does not satisfy Brad's aspiration of seeing the glory of the heavens and the stars. Frost writes,

> We've looked and looked, but after all where are we?
>
> Do we know any better where we are,
>
> And how it stands between the night tonight
>
> And a man with a smoky lantern chimney?
>
> How different from the way it ever stood?

The farmer with the Star-Splitter sees individual stars more perfectly, but he does not see the beauty of the heavens in all their resplendent majesty. With the best telescope he sees only parts of the stars "split" into units but not the constellations or pictures in the sky with their stories. He sacrifices the whole for the part, burning his home for a mere possession—the latest technology—and compromising morality by deliberately setting fire to the house for the sake of the money and cheating the insurance company. Seeing with two human eyes comprehends more of reality, both the heavens above and the earth below, than gazing into the opening of the telescope that presents a piece of a star that is only one part of the cosmos. Brad's far-sightedness is a disorder that needs correction. He does not see more or know more for all his grandiose plans.

In Act II of Shakespeare's *The Tempest* a shipwrecked crew that expected to perish in the storm finds itself safely ashore on land, but the survivors give two different accounts of their escape from death by drowning. To Gonzalo, an old servant, their escape from the fury of waves and wind is nothing short of providential: "But for the miracle,/ I mean our preservation, few in millions/ Can speak like us." In awe he also marvels at the state of their whitewashed clothes, a fact he repeats at least three times during a conversation: "That our garments, being, as they were, drenched in the sea, hold, notwithstanding, their freshness and glosses, being rather new-dyed than stained with salt water." Gonzalo's fellow travelers, however, do not view their survival as a miraculous wonder, and they ridicule Gonzalo's imaginary interpretation of the events. Cynical and skeptical, they consider Gonzalo a doting fool and tell him to stop babbling and exaggerating: "Prithee, peace." Even when Gonzalo notices the pristine beauty of the island ("How lush and lusty the grass looks! How green!"), Antonio and Sebastian mock his simple-mindedness: "The ground indeed is tawny." As the play illustrates, Gonzalo—without any knowledge of Prospero's existence on the island or his magic as the cause of these miracles—has indeed seen the hand of Divine Providence deliver the voyagers from death—the work of Prospero's art that has both caused the tempest and rescued them from drowning in order to bring good out of evil and temper justice with mercy. Gonzalo, pure of heart, sees the goodness and beauty of the island and the mystery behind their escape from death which the other survivors, cruel and hardhearted, cannot perceive.

Seeing in this play is an act of contemplation that beholds the true, the good, and the beautiful that inhere in the natural world of the island and dwell in the hearts and souls of the pure and the good. Prospero, once the Duke of Milan overthrown by his brother Antonio and set adrift on the ocean aboard a "A rotten carcass of a butt, not rigged,/ Nor tackle, sail, nor mast," also escaped from death through a miracle. As he tells the story of his survival to his daughter Miranda, he uses language similar to Gonzalo's words when she asks, "How came we ashore?" Prospero replies, "By providence divine. Some food we had, and some fresh water, that a noble Neapolitan, Gonzalo, /Out of his charity . . . did give us. . . ." While Gonzalo and Prospero attribute their deliverance from death to a miracle, other mariners do not see the whitewashed garments, the pristine beauty of the island, or the hand of Divine Providence. Their reaction to the events is blind to these mysteries that are open secrets, half revealed and half concealed in the manner of camouflage. To Antonio and Sebastian all is blind chance without rhyme or reason. The fact that many do not see does not negate the reality of the miracle and the hand of Providence. To see, then, is to discover the first principles of things and to detect the cause behind the effect.

Seeing in *The Tempest*, to use the language of classical philosophy, is to discover *form* in *matter*, the hidden potentiality that inheres in things and shines out just as Michelangelo said he saw the statue of David in a rock. The spiritual realities of truth, goodness, and beauty shine through the veil of the material, physical, and visible world. Prospero sees Ariel imprisoned in a tree—the form of the spirit hidden in the matter of the tree. Prospero contemplates the miracle of good coming out of evil when he and Miranda do not perish but find a haven on the island. Gonzalo too beholds all the signs of the hand of Divine Providence as he marvels at the abundance of the island. Ferdinand and Miranda fall in love at first sight as they see the divine in human form, contemplating each other's physical beauty as a mirror of the radiance of the soul. Ferdinand marvels at the miracle of woman's physical and spiritual beauty: "Admired Miranda! Indeed the top of admiration! . . . Full many a lady/ I have eyed with best regard. . . . But you, oh, you, /So perfect and so peerless, are created/ Of every creature's best." Miranda sees the image of God in Ferdinand: "I might call him/A thing divine, for nothing natural/ I ever saw so noble." Seeing the form in matter, recognizing spiritual realities through visible signs, and sensing the supernatural by means of the natural all represent the highest levels of seeing and knowing.

True seeing also is the ability to use the good judgment that makes vital distinctions. In Shakespeare's *King Lear* Kent, the devoted servant, tells the king, "See better, Lear." The king fails to distinguish between praise and flattery, between quantity and quality, and between loving a father and loving a husband. When he enjoins his daughters to express the quantity of their love for him before dividing his inheritance ("Which of you shall we say doth love us most?"), Goneril and Regan, the two older daughters, boast that they love Lear "Dearer than eyesight, space, and liberty, /Beyond what can be valued, rich or rare." Cordelia, offended by the bombastic language of her sisters, says simply, "I love your majesty/ According to my bond, nor more nor less." How can Goneril and Regan love their father "all" Cordelia asks. As married women, she explains, they will naturally bestow half their love, care, and duty upon their husbands. No daughter can love a father like a husband or adore a father as if he were a god. Because Cordelia speaks truthfully in measured words instead of pompous rhetoric, she is banished with no inheritance. Her simple declaration of love states, "You have begot me, bred me, loved me. I/ Return those duties back as are right fit,/ Obey you, love you, honor you." Cordelia loves, honors, and respects her father with filial devotion and renders her father his due, but she distinguishes between feigned love and true affection, between profuse words and loving deeds. She differentiates between the degrees of love and acknowledges the hierarchy of relationships that makes justice proportionate rather than quantitative. What is due to a father is not the same as what is due to a husband. While Lear's idea of justice proposes a division of his lands into three equal parts, the fact that each daughter will inherit one-third of his property belies the fact that each portion may not possess the same value. True seeing detects the degrees and gradations that differentiate things.

This tendency to reduce or level essential differences blurs the meaning of justice. Like Lear for whom love is a matter of "how much" rather than "to whom," Edmund, the illegitimate son of Gloucester, also invokes the idea of sameness or equality as the criterion of justice. Comparing his condition of "illegitimate" son to his brother's "legitimate" status, Edmund protests the injustice of the law that does not allow an illegitimate son to inherit his father's fortune. In his eyes there is no essential distinction between him and his half-brother Edgar:

> Why bastard? Wherefore base?
>
> When my dimensions are as well compact as,
>
> My mind as generous and my shape as true,
>
> As honest madam's issue? Why brand they us with
>
> With base? With baseness? Bastardy? (I. ii. 6-9)

In Edmund's eyes the legal distinction between legitimate and illegitimate is arbitrary and illogical, nothing more than "the plague of custom" having no basis in nature because he is endowed with the same natural gifts of mind and body as his brother Edgar. To label the difference between legitimate and illegitimate a more legal convention, however, eliminates the difference between love and lust, between fathering children responsibly within marriage in love and fathering children irresponsibly outside of marriage in promiscuity. Civilization depends upon the defense of these natural distinctions that preserve the moral order, and human wisdom sees clearly what Lear cannot distinguish.

Once Goneril and Regan inherit Lear's wealth by their extravagant declarations of love, they no longer honor him as either king or father. When Lear expects to be welcomed at their castles with his retinue, his daughters protest that he does not need a procession of attendants and servants. Instead of his one hundred retainers, they will allow only fifty, then twenty-five, then ten, and finally five. Goneril and Regan finally conclude that Lear needs no servants: "What need you five and twenty, ten, or five, /To follow in a house where twice so many/ Have a command to tend you?" When Lear is denied the honor of a king and the respect due to a father who reminds his daughters, "I gave you all," he compares a king's presence without servants to a woman's appearance without finery and jewelry. When the daughters insist that Lear does not need a multitude of attendants, he replies that Regan and Goneril also do not need the many articles of apparel they are wearing that serve no utilitarian purpose. The dignity of human beings demands more than the meager necessities for bare survival. The adornment and beautification of human beings carries symbolic meaning, a meaning that true seeing recognizes:

Our basest beggars

Are in the poorest thing superfluous.

Allow not nature more than nature needs,

Man's life's as cheap as beast's. Thou art a lady.

If only to go warm were gorgeous,
Why, nature needs not what thou gorgeous wear'st

Which scarcely keeps thee warm. (II. iv.
267-273)

To fail to distinguish between necessary clothes for work
and elegant attire for formal occasions is to obliterate the
difference between man and animals. "Man's life's cheap
as beasts" when fathers and kings are leveled to mere
men, when beautiful women wear only work clothes
but cannot dress with elegance, when the meanings of
"legitimate" and "illegitimate" are indistinguishable,
and when fulsome lies and truthful words are confused.
"See better, Lear" identifies the problem of blind human
beings ignoring or attempting to undo the logical, natural
distinctions that inhere in the structure of reality.

While Brad McLaughlin's telescope produced the
problem of far-sightedness at the expense of common
sense and down-to earth realism, Jonathan Swift's
Lilliputians in Part I of *Gulliver's Travels* see with myopic
vision: "They see with great Exactness, but at no great
distance." The Lilliputians' nearsightedness corresponds
to their exacting attention to details, measurements, and
minutiae—a narrow-mindedness that fails to see the
whole. An odd race whose average height is six inches
and a people terrified of Gulliver's height and weight,
the Lilliputians spy into Gulliver's pockets, examine his
nostrils, and see the marks on his face, but they do not
see in Gulliver the form of a human being, only a "Man
Mountain," a beast of burden to be used as a slave, and
as a military instrument to conquer their enemies in
war. The diminutive size of the Lilliputians corresponds
to their small-mindedness. Petty in their politics, the
factions in government, the High-Heels and the Low-
Heels, bicker over the size of shoes. They wage war with

Blefuscu because of a dispute about the proper way of breaking of eggs, a bitter feud between the Big-Endians and the Low-Endians. Mean-spirited and vindictive, the self-centered Lilliputians only act on the motive of self-interest, always calculating their gains and losses as clever mathematicians. Because Gulliver poses a physical threat by his gigantic strength and raises concern about famine because of the quantity of food he consumes, the Lilliputians ponder Gulliver's fate by a calculation of profit-loss arithmetic. For these little tyrants the end justifies the means, and their idea of seeing is based exclusively on mathematical reasoning.

While Gulliver's death threatens pestilence because of his enormous corpse, Gulliver's usefulness as an efficient means of transportation, as a weapon of war, and as a powerful labor-saving machine offers benefits to the Lilliputians' self-serving ends. Their high councils of government resolve to keep Gulliver alive but to blind him so that he can be the perfect slave and execute all the commands of his oppressors: "That the Loss of your Eyes would be no impediment to your bodily Strength, by which you might still be useful to his Majesty. That blindness is an addition to Courage, by concealing Dangers from us." Thus the small size and nearsightedness of the Lilliputians signify narrow-mindedness, self-interest, petty revenge, and quarrelsome littleness. In their pride they see themselves as the center of the universe. Swift satirizes a race of people who see all persons as objects to be used, who see reality only in quantitative terms, who use their knowledge of mathematics and science for destructive purposes, who conduct all their affairs exclusively for their own gain and advantage, and who

see only the body of another human being but never the
soul.

Another failure in seeing the true nature of things
and the way things are assumes the form of fantasizing
and daydreaming that Dr. Johnson in *Rasselas* calls "the
dangerous prevalence of imagination." Throughout the
book he satirizes a type of thinker called a "projector"
who dwells on the heights of mountains, lives in
towering observatories, or thinks in terms of vague
abstractions divorced from reality. These thinkers
let "airy notions," "the power of fiction," "silent
speculation," and "visionary schemes" unleash their
uncontrollable imagination that leads to "hope or fear
beyond sober probability" and to naïve theories about
human happiness. One of these projectors fantasizes that
man can learn to fly like birds just as man can swim
like fish. Designing wings, jumping from a height above
a lake, and propelling the wings, he attempts to float
in the air when he suddenly plunges into the water and
narrowly escapes from drowning. An astronomer with
great learning who lives in an observatory imagines that
he controls Mother Nature: "I have possessed for five
years the regulation of the weather and the distribution
of the seasons." A philosopher who discourses on "The
Happiness of a Life Led According to Nature" offers this
tortured explanation of his meaning: "To live according
to nature is to act always with due regard to the fitness
arising from the relations and qualities of causes and
effects; to concur with the great and unchangeable scheme
of universal felicity." The jargon and abstractions in this
statement make Prince Rasslas conclude that this thinker
was "one of the sages whom he should understand less

as he heard him longer." These characters see only what they wish as "fictions begin to operate as realities."

In their lofty positions of eminence situated at the top, these thinkers need to come down to earth. In love with untested theories, simplistic ideas, and vague generalizations, they fail to test theory with practice and temper abstractions with experience. They fail to see the correlation between intellectual notions and concrete things. True seeing is the ability to relate the universal to the particular and the general to the specific. When Rasselas leaves the comfort of the Happy Valley and begins his quest for "the choice of life" to discover the truth about human happiness, he begins with an idealism that his actual experience contradicts. As he anticipates great adventures and heroic undertakings, he imagines that "his benevolence always terminated his projects in the relief of distress, the detection of fraud, the defeat of oppression, and the diffusion of happiness." However, in his actual travels and encounters with people from all social classes and professions, Rasselas never experiences this utopian version of happiness. The hard truth he encounters a number of times is the lesson that "Human life is everywhere a state in which much is to be endured, and little to be enjoyed." True seeing, then, avoids the two extremes of lofty generalizations that ignore particulars and the accumulation of insignificant details that lead to no universal truths. The special gift of the poet, Rasselas learns from the sage Imlac, is the ability "to examine not the individual but the species; to remark general properties and large appearances; he does not number the streaks of the tulip or describe the different shades in the verdure of the forest." The vision of great writers is "conversant with all that is awfully vast or elegantly little" and capable of relating universal truths to particular situations and recognizing in specific examples general laws. This integration of the one and the many is the ability that distinguishes the poet's ability to grasp "right and wrong in their abstracted and invariable state" and to ascend "to general and transcendental truths, which will always be the same."

Human beings need to see with human eyes in a peripheral vision and not equate true perception with telescopic or microscopic seeing. Human eyes in their roundedness are designed to see the whole, not to split images like Brad McLaughlin's "Star-Splitter." The eyes provide not only sight but also insight, the power of seeing into things with penetration and discovering the form in the matter. The more one sees, the better one's judgment if a person both detects analogies and discerns differences. Seeing is not closing one's eyes and making pictures in the mind with an idle imagination but observing the nature of things as they are and have always been. In John Ruskin's words, "The greatest thing a human soul ever does in this world is to see something, and tell what he saw in a plain way. Hundreds of people can talk for one who can think, but thousands can think for one who can see. To see clearly is poetry, prophecy, religion—all in one."

Chapter 17. Personal Acts and the Human Touch

A human being is a person, and his actions are intended to be human, personal acts—not cold, impersonal, insensitive, or unfeeling responses to other persons. Because human beings interact, communicate, speak, and write, these activities all require the sensitive, human touch to make them special. No person wishes to be treated as a statistic, as an anonymous member of a crowd, or in a dehumanized manner that dishonors his dignity and value. No one enjoys making telephone calls and never speaking to human voices. No one takes pleasure in going to the mail box and never receiving a personalized, handwritten letter from a friend or relative. No one values the quality of a life dominated by the routine of work without the personal experiences of friendship, hospitality, and conversation that enrich civilized life. Man is not born to work without play, to live without personal relationships, or to experience a life devoid of the special, touches that fill daily existence with the taste and sweetness of goodness.

For all the electronic communication technology of E-Mail, iPods, instant messaging, chat rooms, voice mail, and information networks, modern life has lost its human touch and its personal voice. Human acts have been replaced by mechanical operations, and personal relationships suffer because of modern man's reliance upon electronic devices and machines for entertainment and pleasure rather than the arts of enjoying people, cultivating hospitality, and forming close friendships. The more that people stare into screens and monitors, the more they rely upon Hollywood and television for entertainment. The more they use cell phones, iPods, and iTunes as essential activities—the less people participate in the humanizing, civilizing activities that bless and enrich the quality of life. No one can "taste and see the sweetness of the Lord," feel touched by the heartwarming hospitality of generous hosts, know the experience of friendship as "the wine of life" in Dr. Johnson's famous phrase, or sense the depths of human relationships or human experiences when enslaved by the bondage of modern communications technology.

What is a person? Unlike animals, persons possess depths which words like the soul, the conscience, and the heart express. The natural human desire is to experience life in its depths—to know the innocent joys of childhood, to experience loyal friendships that span a lifetime, to know the indissoluble bonds of marriage, and to feel an intimacy with God. Human beings are created to know, to love, and to enjoy life at its best which is called civilization and to experience beatitude in heaven which is called Paradise. As Christ said, He came into the world so that man's life would be "full" and "abundant". The revolution in technology that has equipped everyone with more access to media also has isolated persons from other human beings and stunted their social skills. If one is always speaking on a cell phone, playing a video game, surfing on the Internet, texting. or watching television, then of course one does not take a personal interest in other people—whether it is a fellow student, a colleague, family member, or guests. If a person is always too busy or too preoccupied in his attachment to these modern devices, then he does not plumb depths of human experience.

All the quintessential human experiences that offer this personal, life-giving touch are arts which require time and effort to cultivate. They resist the superficiality of instant communication, brief exchanges, rushed conversations, and cold responses. To learn an art—whether it is the art of letter writing, conversation, hospitality, or enjoyment of people—takes a person into his own depths and requires him to consider other people also as having a soul, heart, conscience, and humanity. These arts cultivate the gift of pleasing others by thoughtful gestures of civility and offers of friendliness. One can ignore people or enjoy people; one can take an interest in another person's stories and background or assume his life lacks all human importance; one can appreciate the charm, amiability, goodness, beauty, or wisdom of others or regard them as unappealing or uninteresting. All the traditional social arts begin with the self-evident truth that others possess depth and dignity because they are created in the image of God and possess unique gifts for the enrichment and blessing of others.

Contrast the art of letter writing with the messaging of E-Mail. In composing a letter, a person must create an atmosphere of leisure, evoke the presence of the person receiving the letter and properly address him or her according to the particular occasion, find appropriate topics of general interest, select an appropriate stationery that reflects good taste, use handwriting that reveals individuality and possesses beauty and legibility, and write in a natural tone of affability and courtesy that is measured and balanced—neither solemnly formal nor flippantly casual. In short, a letter requires the observance of etiquette, sensitivity in pleasing and honoring others, a respect for manners, and the virtue of self-possession. A person must rise to the occasion of letter writing just as a person must dress properly for a special occasion or behave courteously in mixed company and polite society. The nature of E-Mail and instant messaging is informal and casual, all the rules relaxed and bent to allow total permissiveness. It is commonplace to receive messages without greetings or salutations, capitalization or punctuation, correct spelling or proofreading. Just as a person dresses tastefully for public occasions out of consideration for others and to avoid giving offense, letter writing demands the same thoughtful sensitivity and respect for others. In the common E-Mail correspondence of academe, teachers often receive messages that begin "Hey professor"—no salutation, no name, no formality, no discrimination. The art of letter writing teaches the human art of "dressing up" for special occasions whereas E-Mail messages encourage "dressing down," poor taste, and slovenly manners.

Consider the art of human conversation in contrast to attachment to the technology of computers, television, smart phones, and iPods. To initiate a conversation signals an interest in another person as a human being, a desire to know a person with greater familiarity, a willingness to learn of another person's background or history, and an openness to learn from the wisdom of others and broaden one's circle of acquaintances. From conversation comes the personal knowledge of lived experience, the proverbial wisdom handed down from generations, and the discovery of another person's interests, ideals, and individuality. Leon Kass in *The Hungry Soul* captures the essence of conversation by recalling its original meanings in Latin and French:

"to turn oneself about" and "to move to and fro"—a turning and a moving which refer to "passing one's life and keeping company with others, toward whom one turns and with whom one moves, sometimes this way, sometimes that." In conversations a person discovers and relishes the unrepeatable uniqueness of other human beings, a quality that Gerard Manley Hopkins called "more distinctive than the taste of ale or alum, more distinctive than the smell of walnutleaf or camphor, and is incommunicable. . ." As the friends of Dr. Johnson said of him at his death, "no man can put you in mind of Johnson"—a trait that his love of conversation impressed upon all who enjoyed his delightful companionship and playful, witty mind. During the exchange of conversation occurs the natural pleasure of giving and receiving, the opening of the heart and the releasing of the spirit that communicates the interior life of another person. The preoccupation with electronic media, on the other hand, separates human beings from the lives and interests of other persons. The main channel of information and stimulation is the visual image on the screen, a medium that obviously does not allow exchange, argument, or debate. In conversation one discerns the difference between the knowledge that lives in people and the information that networks and media disseminate. Without the spontaneous flow of give and take and the honest exchange of thoughts in conversation, a person easily becomes prey for propaganda, ideology, and brainwashing. In C. S. Lewis's *Screwtape Letters* the devils' strategy of propaganda intends to inhibit conversation or argument because "By the very act of arguing, you awake the patient's reason; and once it is awake, who can foresee the result?"

The Christian faith values persons as images of God and respects the sacredness of all life. Christ taught his disciples that their relationship was personal: they were His friends, not His servants, and He opened His mind and heart to His beloved friends: "To you it has been given to know the secrets of the kingdom of heaven. . . ." The Lord and His disciples model this example of personal acts and personal relationships in the many scenes of hospitable eating and drinking they spent in each other's company, in the many conversations they exchanged, in the noble friendship they shared, and of course in The Last Supper. The restoration of Christian culture to an impersonal world demands the cultivation of these lost arts which transform the dreary tedium of monotonous routine into the joy of ordinary living. Notice how the custom of hospitality elevates human life from the struggle for survival to the art of living well in Homer's *Odyssey*: After receiving the kindness of King Alcinous's generous and gracious hospitality, Odysseus remarks, "I feel that there is nothing more delightful than when the festive mood reigns in a whole people's hearts and the banqueters listen to a minstrel from their seats in the hall, while the tables before them are laden with bread and meat, and a steward carries round the wine he has drawn from the bowl and fills their cups. This, to my way of thinking, is something like perfection." These feasts feature many virtues associated with the refinements of civilization. The host pours out libations to the gods as an expression of gratitude for the heavenly gifts of savory food and sparkling wine. The host serves the guest in an environment of elegance and beauty, and the maids serve the visitors with a "beautiful golden ewer" and "the silver basin" that reflect choice dishware made of the best materials and the best craftsmanship. The host practices the virtue of liberality or generosity in preparing the best foods and offering the heartiest portions, sparing nothing for the needs and pleasure of the traveler: "Meanwhile a carver dished up for them on platters slices of various meats he had selected from his board, and put gold cups beside them." These thoughtful gestures and personal touches, then, dignify human life and hint of the divine, "something like perfection".

The elevation of the human spirit to a contemplation of the gods, to a sense of wonder at the reality of beauty, and to an appreciation of the goodness of the human heart, however, mark only part of the occasion. The banquets of hospitality in the *Odyssey* also provide occasions for conversation and storytelling, an opportunity to learn the personal history of the traveler. When Odysseus narrates his adventures with the Cyclops and the Sirens, the feast creates an opportunity for learning and broadening one's mind and for acquiring what Homer calls "the knowledge of men and manners." Entertainment or games also accompany the rituals of hospitality in Greek epic. The bard with his "heavenly gift of delighting our ears whatever theme he chooses for our song," "the perennial delight" of athletic contests, and the performance of the graceful dancers that follow the meal and the conversation all combine to cheer the heart, uplift the soul, and exhilarate the body. They form the art of living well—treating human beings in the most personal, thoughtful, and sensitive of ways. As the practice of old-world hospitality declines and more eating occurs in fast-food restaurants and as homes fail to provide festive occasions where the art of graciousness and pleasing others flourishes, life becomes more impersonal and dehumanized, and the world becomes a colder place. These scenes of hospitality are the natural settings for the art of conversation and the art of enjoying people to flourish. Life always acquires a human touch where friendly conversation flows.

The great Dr. Johnson, eminent man of letters in the eighteenth century, was famous for his great accomplishments as a conversationalist. His many remarks on the topic in Boswell's *Life of Johnson* illuminate the various degrees of conversation and all its varied benefits. First, the simple conversation of affability promotes good will and charity. Sociability does not demand scintillating wit or polished sophistication: "That is the happiest conversation where there is no competition, no vanity, but a calm quiet interchange of sentiments." When Boswell on one occasion complained about the absence of stimulating conversation at a dinner which served a sumptuous banquet, he asked "Why then meet at table?" Johnson answered that good conversation did not demand intellectual substance: "Why, to eat and drink together, and to promote kindness." Boswell's biography records another comment of Johnson that highlights the personal, civilizing dimension of pleasant conversation—not its educational content: "The happiest conversation is that of which nothing is remembered but a general effect of pleasing impression." Besides promoting kindness and friendship, the art of conversation invites playfulness and mirth and develops the sense of wit and laughter. Boswell writes, "He frequently indulged himself in colloquial pleasantry; and the heartiest merriment was often enjoyed in his company." For example, Boswell claimed that David Hume and Samuel Foote boasted that they did not fear death, provoking Johnson's irrepressible wit: "It is not true, Sir. Hold a pistol to Foote's breast, or to Hume's breast, and threaten to kill them, and you'll see how they behave." Johnson then asked Boswell if he would believe anyone putting his hand in a flame and then claiming he felt no pain.

Thus the art of conversation not only cultivates charitable fellowship and innocent laughter but also broadens the mind and cures nonsense. In his conversation Johnson on many occasions exposed what he called "cant," affectations and pretensions which contradicted common sense and defied the wisdom of the world. In one example when Boswell asserted that a life in public affairs would "vex" him extremely if Parliament acted contrary to his wishes, Johnson was unsparing in his rebuttal: "That's cant, Sir. It would not vex you more in the house, than in the gallery. Public affairs vex no man," and he concluded, "My dear friend, clear your mind of cant." Always warning Boswell of the dangers of exaggeration and sentimentality, Johnson told him not to "cant" on behalf of the cult of the noble savage, the idea of primitivism popularized by Rousseau that equated happiness with leaving society and returning to nature: "Do not allow yourself, Sir, to be imposed upon by such gross absurdity. If a bull cold speak, he might as well exclaim,—"Here am I with this cow and this grass; what being can enjoy greater felicity?'" In its natural lighthearted playfulness, the laughter-loving nature of good conversation that is intrinsically enjoyable for its own sake also clears the mind of nonsense and keeps a man from thinking foolishly. Whether the art of conversation promotes kindness, awakens mirth, or engages the mind, it is a quintessential human activity that makes a world of difference between merely living or living well.

When virtual classrooms and on-line "Blackboard" programs replace actual oral communication, the qualities and benefits of good conversation that Johnson relishes are absent from learning, and the human touch is lacking in life. An essential element of a social life and an intellectual life—dialogue—has disappeared. The pure enjoyment of another's personality is never discovered, and the amiability, charm, or mirth in a person's voice or spirit is missed. One of life's exquisite pleasures has been omitted. When family members watch television during their meals and bypass the normal exchanges of conversation about the day's events, natural human interaction suffers. Absent the spirit of old world hospitality and Johnsonian conversation, the joy of discovering another person's family history and the ethnic background of a person's traditions and roots remains unknown. As individuals consume more time attached to electronic devices, the habit of sociable, humanizing civility and graciousness become rare. Fun is no longer spending time with the people who are loved and befriended but an isolated, individualistic activity that never contributes to the happiness of others. The verbal arts of wit, repartee, storytelling, and joking become obsolete without the normal, natural experience of human conversation on a myriad of topics.

Another lost art that needs restoration in the dehumanized, impersonal world is the personal letter with its distinctive handwriting and individual stationery that sparkles like a gem in the collection of the daily mail filled with the usual bills, advertisements, and credit card offers. The personal letter is a reminder that life is not just business or work but also play and delight. Unlike telephone calls, letters allow for re-reading and sharing with others. They possess a taste, flavor, and style which lend themselves to savoring their content and sentiments in a way that telephone calls and e-mail cannot duplicate. The personal touch of letters reassures people that they are unique and special rather than unimportant or nondescript. Someone found the time and took the interest and gave priority to the importance of communicating to a friend, relative, or loved one. Someone realized the importance of the little things that beautify and civilize daily existence. The art of letter writing is a most personal act because it involves imagining the presence of the other person and recalling everything about the person being addressed—his or her character, temperament, sensibility, interests, and background. One must picture being in this person's company and holding a conversation. Letter writing develops in the correspondent the art of pleasing another person by engaging in common topics of interest, displaying a sense of humor, offering wise advice, acknowledging gratitude, or expressing love. Like the art of hospitality and the cultivation of friendship, letter writing requires effort and thoughtfulness, even though it can be lighthearted, whimsical, and informal. Personal letters allow a person to communicate the deepest emotions and the most heartfelt sentiments of the soul and illustrate Cardinal Newman's favorite saying: *Cor ad cor loquitur* (Heart speaks to heart).

For example, John Henry Newman's letter to Henry Manning just prior to the death of Manning's wife illustrates the immense comfort that a letter brings in a time of human tragedy:

It often strikes me so when I am partaking of Holy Communion that I am but drinking in (perchance) temporal sorrow, according to His usual Providence. Hence St. Peter tells us not to think affliction a strange thing. Let us then, my dear Manning, be your comfort,— You are called to trouble as we all are, and the severer the more God loves you. . . . He does not willingly afflict us, nor will put a single grain's weight more of suffering than is meet and good for you to bear—and be sure too that with your suffering your support will grow, and that if in His great wisdom and love He take away the desire of your eyes, it will only be to bring her really nearer to you. For those we love are not nearest to us in the flesh, but they come into our very hearts as being spiritual beings, when they are removed from us. Alas! It is hard to persuade oneself this, when we have the presence and are without the experience of the absence of those we love; yet the absence is often more than the presence, even were this all, that our treasure being removed hence, leads us to think more of Heaven and less of earth.

Because Newman writes to Manning as friend to friend speaking heart to heart, he does not offer false pity, pious clichés, or sentimental cant. The mystery of death and its inconsolable grief move Newman to speak from the depths of his soul and from the riches of his mind. Henry Manning's beloved wife is not eternally absent but more nearly present because she is now a spiritual being rather than a creature of flesh and blood and thus more intimate in the invisible bond of love. Although it taxes the mind to accept this paradox—just as it confuses the intelligence to believe that God ascribes the most severe crosses to those whom He especially loves—these truths make it possible to know peace and joy even in the midst of grave sorrows. The truths expressed in letters can offer solace to the brokenhearted by leading them to the heart of a mystery and illuminating paradoxes that escape conventional opinions.

At a time of great personal crisis when he was approaching death, Dr. Johnson wrote the following letter to the Rev. Dr. Taylor dated April 12, 1784:

> Dear Sir,—What can be the reason that I hear nothing from you? I hope nothing disables you from writing. . . . Do not omit giving me the comfort of knowing, that after all my losses I have yet a friend left. . . . I want every comfort. My life is very solitary and very cheerless. . . . O! my friend, the approach of death is very dreadful. I am afraid to think on that which I know I cannot avoid. It is vain to look round and round for that help which cannot be had. . . . . But let us learn to derive our hope only from God. In the mean time, let us be kind to one another. I have no friend now living but you and Mr. Hector, that was the friend of my youth. Do not neglect, dear Sir, yours affectionately.

Johnson cherishes the letters he receives and anticipates the joys and comforts they bring. Because he suffers from poor health, the gloom of loneliness, and the fear of death, letters from friends epitomize light in the midst of darkness. Striving to practice the supernatural virtue of hope, Johnson utters no pious clichés and feigns no naïve optimism. Like all men, Johnson also must endure the afflictions that attend his own death and enter the dark night of the soul trusting in God's mercy. Letters such as Johnson's acknowledge the human condition and depict the honest thoughts and heartfelt emotions of every person contemplating his own death. The best letters render the authentic taste of reality and lead us to the center of all human lives and to the hearts of others—"the permanent things". Their personal touch allows human beings to enjoy life more and endure life better. More than anything else in the dark night of the soul, Dr. Johnson implores his friend to continue writing letters and cherishes them as medicine for the soul.

Without the restoration of the lost art of letter writing, the noblest sentiments, the wisest advice, the most beautiful love letters, and the most poignant expressions of gratitude will not be recorded. The world will lose some of its most priceless treasures, letters written to beloved people that speak volumes about the graciousness of human hearts. No one prizes telephone calls or values E-mail messages in the way that some letters will be cherished and remembered, read and re-read, marveled at and contemplated again and again for generations and generations. Here is a letter written during the Civil War from Sullivan Ballou to his wife dated July 14, 1861:

Sarah, my love for you is deathless; it seems to bind me with mighty cables that nothing but Omnipotence could break. . . .

But Oh Sarah! If the dead can come to this earth and flit unseen around those they loved, I shall always be near you; in the gladdest days and in the darkest nights. . . Always—Always, and if there be a soft breeze upon your cheek, it shall be my breath, as the cool air fans your throbbing temple, it shall be my spirit passing by. Sarah, do not mourn me dead; think I am gone and wait for thee, for we shall meet again. . . .

As this letter from husband to wife illustrates, a personal letter is always particular; it is written to one person, not to the masses. It addresses a person as a special being, not a member of an audience or a crowd. It expresses the sincerest and purest feelings of the heart in the freshest of ways, not slogans or clichés. Thus the letter becomes precious, a "joy forever" to be cherished for a lifetime and in the course of a family's whole history. Letters, written in the stillness and silence of contemplation, illuminate the great truth that human happiness consists in these relationships that form the highest purposes of life.

A final example of the beauty of the personal touch that is so lacking in modern culture is this letter written by a child to a parent that acknowledges the deepest gratitude for the gift of life and love in the course of a whole lifetime:

Dad, I wanted to thank you from the bottom of my heart for being my father and for all the sacrifices you have made for me. . . . You have taught me so much about life through your example. . . . You have taught me it is more blessed to give than to receive and to strive with all my heart to give back as much as has been given to me. . . .

I am glad you were touched by the wedding—you who only laugh when something is truly funny and compliment when it is truly deserved. Your comment that our dance was "the quintessence of beauty incarnate" was a compliment that exceeded my expectations.

Dad, I love you so much. I always think of you and Mom when I put on my wedding band. Thanks for bequeathing it to me. I cherish it with all my heart.

(Letter of a son to a widowed father, August 31, 2003)

Whether it is the occasion of a man grieving for a dying wife, a friend struggling on his deathbed, a soldier suffering in the midst of war, or a son or daughter rejoicing in the happiness of the wedding, the personal letter transforms the quality of the day and lends it "something like perfection". Lifting, inspiring, or healing the heart, the gracious letter renews a person's love of life and gladdens the human spirit. To live well, to rejoice always, and to think of the highest things, the things that are above, and to be reminded of the glory of being human, man needs to give and receive in the form of letters just as he needs to give and receive in the form of friendship, conversation, and hospitality.

All these activities—festive occasions of hospitality, the enjoyment of conversation and people in the spirit of friendship, and the custom of letter writing—are pursued and enjoyed for their own sake, as ends in themselves. They are intrinsically good and desirable for their own sake, not as a means to an end. They all belong to the realm of play and leisure rather than work and business. Because they all appear to be time-consuming, deliberate, unhurried activities compared to instant messaging, Internet speed, and electronic communications, they seem to be wastes of time when faster means are available. However, in a sentence from Saint Exupery's *The Little Prince*, "It is only the time we 'waste' with our friends that counts." As Father James V. Schall explains in *On the Unseriousness of Human Affairs*,

> To waste our time with our friends means that we do not have some sort of tight agenda, that we are not always looking at our watches or worrying about our lives. . . . We need time-out-of-time, the time that passes without our noticing. Someone needs to protect us from the urgency of immediate things. We need a kind of escape from what everyone takes to be our main tasks.

The quintessential human acts that are personal all possess this trait of creating time from work and busyness for occasions of joy that offer physical rejuvenation and spiritual renewal—occasions that evoke gratitude, love, hope, and wonder at "all that is given to us, all that is," to use Father Schall's words. To restore a Christian culture that gives glory to God for all the small and great blessings of the gift of life, the civilizing arts of hospitality, friendship, conversation, the enjoyment of people, and letter writing need cultivation and preservation in an age that is too rushed, too unfriendly, too impersonal, and too inhospitable.

Chapter 18. Motion and Rest in Frost's Poetry: Stopping, Pausing, Rushing, and Traveling

In many of his poems Robert Frost portrays moments in which busy human beings stop in the middle of a day's work or a long journey. Even during a leisurely walk on a familiar path with no new sights there is an occasion to pause, reflect, or contemplate. During these times when workers or travelers relax, linger, and turn their attention to the sights or sounds around them that do not relate to the purpose of their work or journey, they experience a moment of gratitude, feel the power of beauty, sense the wonder of love, or know the reality of God's presence. Something illuminating happens when persons learn to be still and notice the world that surrounds them. They hear voices or receive messages or gain clarity in a most human, natural, and yet mysterious way that validates their efforts and renews their hearts and spirits. To be human is to know how to stop and be willing to rest instead of merely traveling a certain number of miles per hour to reach a destination and finish a task in the shortest time. Human beings move in a way that distinguishes their nature as rational, reflective beings who desire to know and love the truth—a motion that has nothing in common with the movement of horses and ants that Frost describes as restless or impatient.

In "Stopping by Woods on a Snowy Evening" a man traveling by horse pauses on his journey to behold the beauty of the winter evening and the silence of the night during a gentle snowfall. Marveling at the beauty of his surroundings, he stops his travel to gaze in wonder at the purity and quiet of the scene, a delay that disorients the horse: "My little horse must think it queer/ To stop without a farmhouse near/ Between the woods and frozen lake/ The darkest evening of the year." Horses do not wonder at beauty, stop for recollection, or meditate on the purpose of life or the meaning of life's journey. Man by nature is a contemplative being for whom beauty leads to truth and for whom wonder is the beginning of knowledge. To stop for no urgent reason in the middle of the journey when many miles of road lie ahead and when a horse "gives his harness bells a shake/ To ask if there is some mistake" reveals man's need to ponder and reflect about the destination and the end of human activity. To be still, to have wonder, and to know renew the mind and heart to commit and persevere in completing the duties of one's vocation: "The woods are lovely, dark, and deep, / But I have promises to keep, /And miles to go before I sleep/ And miles to go before I sleep." Stopping by woods and listening to "the sweep of /Of easy wind and downy flake" makes a person receptive to other sounds like the whisperings of the heart and the voice of conscience that speak in silence about the duties that honor obliges a person to keep.

In "The Tuft of Flowers" a man arrives to complete the work begun by another laborer: "I went to turn the grass once after one/Who mowed it in the dew before the sun." He finds himself alone on the land, a solitary worker with no human interaction during his day's task of raking. He relates the loneliness of his situation to the isolation of the mower and to the hardship of the human condition: "And I must be, as he had been—alone, /'As all must be,' I said within my heart, / 'Whether they work together or apart.' " As he compares his condition to the lot of the mower and concludes that they are strangers who live in separate, unrelated worlds, he notices a butterfly flying in circles "Seeking . . . Some resting flower of yesterday's delight." Watching the uncertain movements of the butterfly, the raker observes that it finally alights on a tuft of flowers that were not cut by the mower for any other purpose than pure love of their beauty and "from sheer morning gladness at the brim." In his spontaneity the mower had no deliberate intention of letting the flowers bloom for a particular person on the scene, but he had nevertheless communicated with another person and sent "a message from the dawn." The one who came to turn the grass "held brotherly speech" with a stranger he never saw. Like the traveler who stopped to admire the beauty of the woods, the mower found the leisure to be open to the gift of beauty awaiting him.

Because the mower paused and the raker stopped without single-minded fixation on work, the glory of the beautiful spoke to them. Beautiful flowers are a universal language that all men understand. To send flowers to gladden the heart or to beautify the world is the most human of touches, one that requires the thoughtfulness of stopping to think of others and creating the time to fill the day with joy. Stopping, noticing, and listening allow a person to see and hear an eloquent, expressive world that is not a hollow universe but social and communicative in a wordless language of its own for those that have ears to hear and the leisure to enjoy. A tuft of flowers transfigures the world from a solitary, impersonal existence of isolated individuals into a human family that share their happiness because mower and raker give priority to the human and the beautiful over the efficient and the productive.

In "Two Look at Two" a couple in love on an ordinary evening walk see a beautiful sight that touches their hearts and makes them feel in tune with the world, a part of something greater than themselves. Unrushed and strolling, the lovers slowly come to the end of their walk "When they were halted by a tumbled wall/ With barbed-wire binding." Ready to retrace their steps, they utter "Good night to woods" and "This is all." Nothing exceptional or extraordinary interrupts their leisurely walk as they conclude a typical day. Just before they turn to change direction, they notice a doe gazing at them from the opposite side of the wall. Surprisingly, the deer shows no timidity or fear in its silent reaction to the lovers: "She seemed to think that, two thus, they were safe." Two human beings behold with amazement a doe that returns their look with a quiet fascination, not the instinct of panic. When the deer finally moves "unscared along the wall," the couple feels privileged to have witnessed a rare sight. Grateful for this glimpse into a secret, the lovers respond, "*This*, then is all." They received an unexpected gift, a special grace, something extra or in addition that a walk in the woods ordinarily does not offer. Mother Nature speaks to their hearts because they were in a state of peace, recollection and serenity that opens the mind to hear the messages that are whispered or to behold the beautiful revelations that are unveiled.

Assuming the evening has concluded and ready to return, the lovers witness another sight that astonishes them. This time a buck arrives along the wall and gazes at the man and woman with the same steady look as the doe's glance, "as if to ask, 'Why don't you make some motion?/ Or give some sign of life? Because you can't. / I doubt if you're as living as you look." Neither man nor deer want to break the magical spell that captures the quintessence of love. Love has been felt, communicated, and exchanged in its giving, in its "twoness." A man and a woman on one side of the wall and a doe and buck on the other side see a reflection, a mirror of the bond that unites male and female in the great law of love that circulates throughout all of creation in the form of an endless cycle of mutual giving and receiving that is inexhaustible in its fullness. After this moment of revelation and awe, the couple's response is "This *must* be all." A simple walk at night has unveiled a mystery as they contemplate the beauty and goodness of love that speaks everywhere:

> Still they stood,
>
> A great wave from it going over them,
>
> As if the earth in one unlooked for favor
>
> Had made them certain earth returned their love.

Spellbound and awed, touched and moved, humbled and thankful, the couple receive not merely something or "all" but "more" than they imagined or expected. They gain not merely the pleasantness of a calm night or feel the closeness of the bond of love but receive a precious gift, "an unlooked-for favor"—a glimpse into the heart of love as a constant exchange and reciprocal giving, a glance into the greatness of a love that fills all of creation and responds with "a great wave" from the heart of reality. Their quiet, leisurely walk made them receptive to the beauty of love that surrounded them.

In "The Mountain" Frost depicts two types of travelers, an old man who has lived at the base of Mount Hor but never climbed to the summit and a young traveler full of ambition to climb to the top. The old man admits, "I've been on the sides, /Deer-hunting and trout-fishing" and "It doesn't seem so much to climb a mountain/ You've worked around all your life." He has traveled around the mountain many times at a natural pace but never felt an impetuous urge to scale the heights. Approaching the old man to inquire about the best path to reach the top, the mountain climber notices the deliberate, unhurried pace of the man on a wagon: "And there I met a man who moved so slow/ With white-faced oxen, in a heavy cart." On the other hand, the young visitor has fixed his mind on the bold adventure of an athletic feat. Appearing in a rush, he asks questions in a curt manner that seeks immediate information: "What town is this?" "Is that the way to reach the top from here?" "You've never climbed it?" "You never saw it?" "Can one walk around it?" "You've lived here all your life?" Frost contrasts the older man's slow movements in traveling around the mountain many times and the tourist's hasty zeal in finding the most direct path that leads to the end—the difference between many concentric circles around the mountain and a straight line to the top and the bottom in one trip. The old man's leisurely rhythm and normal pace have bestowed a wisdom about Mount Hor that a day's adventure to the summit cannot achieve.

Frost shows the world of difference between the wisdom which the old man has slowly acquired over time and the information the young newcomer seeks in the course of the day. While the wise man offers to the impatient tourist all the wisdom of his experience about the mountain in the form of stories and anecdotes, the young traveler only asks for factual information and "yes" and "no" answers. How can a man know everything about the top of the mountain if he has never traveled there? The wise man refers to a spring or fountain at the heights of the mountain but admits he never saw it and describes the water as "Warm in December, cold in June"—statements that make no sense to the mountain climber who acts skeptical about a mountain no one has seen ("If it's there") and about a remark that makes no sense to him (water warm in winter and cold in summer?). Wisdom grasps paradoxes that information does not comprehend—ideas like Heraclitus's famous saying that "the way up is the way down" or St. Paul's statement that "the invisible things of God" are known by "the visible." Without ascending to the heights the wise man knows much about the top of the mountain because he has lived and traveled and circulated around Mount Hor during the entire course of a lifetime. Without actually seeing the source of the water from exploring above, he knows that all effects resemble their causes:

> I guess there's no doubt
>
> About its being there. I never saw it.
>
> It may not be right on the very top:
>
> It wouldn't have to be a long way down
>
> To have some head of water from above,

And a good distance down might not be noticed

By anyone who'd come a long way up.

Thus the gradual, leisurely, patient movements of the man "who moved so slow" affords him a knowledge of the whole which the great mountain represents. His mode of travel allows him an understanding of the entirety of Mount Hor both above and below and from side to side and in its seen and unseen aspects. Going around and around a subject by way of travel, experience, or conversation eventually leads to the heart of the matter or the essence of truth, an understanding of the whole and its parts, the one and the many. On the other hand, moving directly and quickly in a straight path to and from the summit of knowledge may offer a view from the top that sees the outward and the exterior but does not detect the hidden wonder or underlying mystery. The mountain climber says, "There ought to be a view around the world/ From such a mountain." But this panoramic view that can see for miles never knows the secrets about the deer hunting and the trout fishing and the brook at the top. Frost shows that leisure prepares for wisdom and haste repels it.

Frost portrays another kind of unspectacular, unadventurous form of movement in "The Road Not Taken." The traveler must choose between two diverging roads that look equally attractive and beckoning, lamenting "And sorry I could not travel both/ And be one traveler." These two roads do not present a choice similar to Christ's parable about the narrow gate that leads to heavenly joy and the broad highway that leads to damnation. The two roads in Frost's poem appear indistinguishable. Just when one of the roads seems to have the slight advantage of "having perhaps the better claim, /Because it was grassy and wanted wear," the distinction disappears and makes the decision more difficult: "Though as for that, the passing there/Had worn them equally about the same, /And both that morning equally lay/ In leaves no step had trodden black." Comparing and contrasting the two options provides no clarity or discernment of the better choice because no subtle but vital distinction emerges. Yet the traveler does finally select one of the roads but decides by way of chance rather than by calculation and acts without a sense of certainty or foresight: "Oh, I kept the first for another day!/ Yet knowing how way leads on to way,/ I doubted if I should ever come back." Imagining the consequences of his choice and the end of the road he pursued, the traveler speculates, "I shall be telling this with a sigh/ Somewhere ages and ages hence: / Two roads diverged in a wood, and I—/I took the one less traveled by."

The critical decision, then, does not lie between the two roads that are both appealing but in the commitment to the chosen path as it mysteriously unfolds as "way leads on to way." To be steadfast, persevering, and dedicated from beginning to end on the course one has chosen is the element that has "made all the difference"— not the less traveled road. To decide on the basis of an intuition or by a feeling of the heart rather than on the basis of a guarantee or proof also has "made all the difference" as it shows a willingness to take a chance and be adventurous. To choose one road that naturally excludes the second choice also makes all the difference because it demonstrates honesty and realism, the fact that one cannot travel both roads, that "one cannot have his cake and eat it too." In short, to act according to the best lights a person has, to take a chance, to make a commitment, to finish the journey, and to trust in Divine Providence offer the best explanation of the traveler's success—not his far-reaching wisdom or great prudence about the future. His way of travel, though adventurous, was not whimsical, erratic, impulsive, or irrational but human, natural, and orderly as one thing leads to another "knowing how way leads on to way."

Contrary to these natural ways of moving and stopping, working and resting, walking and taking one's time, thinking and deciding, and committing and persevering, Frost in "Departmental" satirizes efficient bureaucracy for its perfunctory, impersonal procedure in conducting business that resembles the regimentation of an ant colony. Nothing interrupts the order of the ant colony as the insects march with perfect precision. Accidents, emergencies, and deaths do not interfere with the day's business:

An ant on the tablecloth

Ran into a dormant moth

Of many times his size.

He showed not the least surprise.

His business wasn't with such.

The ant communicates the accidental death to another ant assigned to "the hive's enquiry squad" who specializes in emergencies. Another ant, encountering the death of a fellow ant from the colony and following the chain of command, signals to the court to remove the body:

"Death's come to Jerry McCormic,

Our selfless forager Jerry.

Will the special Janizary

Whose office it is to bury

The dead of the commissary

Go bring him home to his people."

Without pause, delay, or complications the industrious ants conduct their busy work with proficient dispatch and pragmatic organization, never wasting time or duplicating effort and never deviating from the line of duty.

With clocklike regularity they move, communicate, delegate, and remove obstacles or problems that pose a threat to the perfect functioning of their expert efficiency. After news of Jerry's death is instantly reported to the queen, she commissions the business to the funeral director in charge of this specialization: "And presently on the scene/ Appears a solemn mortician,/ With feelers calmly twiddle,/ Seizes the dead by the middle,/ Heaving him high in the air,/ Gets him out of there." Functioning mechanically in rote-like movements with no emotion and no thought—neither tears, sympathy, nor sadness— the ants conduct their work in the most dehumanized and insensitive of manners. They accomplish their business, achieve results, and leave nothing unfinished or imperfect in their day's activity. The ants do no evil, commit no violence, and cause no trouble: "It couldn't be called ungentle./ But how thoroughly departmental." In other words, they have no human touch, no human heart, and no compassion. When human beings, businesses and organizations perform their work with only the goals of productivity, cost effectiveness, efficiency, and profit in mind at the expense of the moral sentiments and the virtues of the heart, then men reduce themselves to robots and machines for whom performance outweighs humanity.

Frost's poetry never loses sight of the small things, humble work, and simple ways of ordinary life that give it an exquisitely personal and human dimension that uplifts it from the humdrum, prosaic quality of daily existence. A long journey with a stop in the woods to marvel at the pristine beauty of a snowfall comes as a heaven-sent gift of inspiration. A glance at a tuft of flowers while working alone in the field transforms a lonely, dreary day into a moment of pure joy between a mower and a raker. A walk in the evening leads a man and a woman to see a doe and buck gaze at them as two look at two—the lovers in awe at the spellbound moment of deer communicating to human beings the essence of love's mystery and the deer enchanted by the sight of two persons whom they view as natural friends, not enemies. A traveler chooses a road by casual accident that leads to a destiny and a human journey full of surprises, a stroke of luck more than a reward for hard work. Frost shows the importance of the little things that lead to the great things: a stop in the woods, a tuft of flowers, the sight of deer on a walk, and a journey down a road all begin in the heart of everyday life but transcend ordinary experience. The simple leads to the great, the natural to the mysterious, the visible to the invisible, and the accidental to the providential if one moves, feels, or reacts in a truly human way.

The way one moves makes all the human difference in the world. If a man rushes like a horse and does not pause for the contemplation of beauty; if a man views his day as merely the drudgery of the sweat of the brow and finds no delight around him and spreads no cheer anywhere; if a person with great aspirations has no time for conversation with older, wiser people because of his ambition for achievement; or if someone works like a drudge or a drone with no reactions to the drama of love, luck, suffering, and death, then life turns into a journey that goes nowhere, man exists only to work and survive, the poetry and romance of life have no reality, and all of life becomes "departmental."

Chapter 19. Old-World Manners in Today's World: Marriage in Jane Austen's Novels

Jane Austen's novels immediately introduce readers to the central theme of her books, the importance of marriage in a person's life and the blessings it brings as life's greatest source of human happiness when men and women choose spouses on the basis of love, attraction, reason, and moral principles. The opening line of *Pride and Prejudice* is famous: "It is a truth universally acknowledged, that a single man in possession of a good fortune, must be in want of a wife." In *Emma* marriage exerts a powerful appeal for Mr. Knightley because "There was too much domestic happiness in his brother's house; woman wore too amiable a form in it." Emma regards Harriet Smith as an admirable woman who offers "all the best blessings of existence" to the husband who marries her. In Austen's novels, however, all the happiness of marriage awaits only those who marry for the right reasons—those who conduct a proper courtship prior to marriage that reveals to the man and woman the heart, soul, and moral character of the person they are considering for marriage and those whose manners reveal them as persons of charity, honor, and magnanimity. In *Pride and Prejudice* Mr. Collins' three proposals in the course of a month to Jane Bennet, Elizabeth Bennet, and Charlotte Lucas blatantly disregard the stage of courtship as he views matrimony as a mark of social respectability and public approval important to his status as an Anglican clergyman. In the same novel Mr. Wickham's elopement with Lydia causes shock and scandal because both persons have shown no romantic interest in the other except for Lydia's flirtations with the soldiers. Marriage without courtship leads to marital relationships governed exclusively by economic and social considerations or by the need to avoid humiliation and shame.

Courtship in Austen's novels depends on social occasions—dances, assemblies, dinner parties, visits, and outings—where men and women receive introductions, initiate friendships, enjoy conversation, display manners, and receive first impressions. Jane and Bingley's romance in *Pride and Prejudice* begins at the Netherfield Ball, Elizabeth and Darcy's love begins in her visit to his estate at Pemberley Woods, and Mr. Knightley's relationship with Emma grows because of their longstanding friendship and the many times he visits the Woodhouse home. These social occasions provide natural opportunities for exchange and interaction that can cultivate relationships and awaken romantic interest. Courtship does not happen in a vacuum, and it is not a result of clever manipulation. In Emma the heroine learns with great embarrassment that all her efforts to match the simple Harriet Smith with the sophisticated Mr. Elton or to contrive a romance between the ingenuous Harriet and deceitful Frank Churchill fail because these couples do not discover each other in the natural settings of normal social life. Mr. Collins' formal visit to the Bennets to select a wife in the course of a few weeks also lacks the proper context of men and women meeting and becoming acquainted in a spontaneous and uncontrived way, and Darcy's meddlesomeness in Mr. Bingley's growing attachment to Jane Bennet also spoils the course of true love that begins in a normal way. Courtship, then, originates in sociability, the coming and going of families and friends who join each other on a host of occasions where people freely mix and mingle.

These social events in Austen's novels, however, prescribe a code of propriety and civility that makes them pleasant, agreeable occurrences for all parties. Without the ideal of good manners social situations would be unwelcome events that would spoil the festive nature of neighbors gathering for the dance or for dinner. Manners, however, are not superficial amenities in these novels, and manners are not mere rules, perfunctory rituals, or cold formalities. In all of Austen's works true manners embody acts of charity, tactful graciousness, and special acts of thoughtfulness that elevate human beings as magnanimous persons. In *Emma* Austen praises Mrs. Weston's impeccable sense of decorum and good taste as manners that reflect not only propriety but also "simplicity" and "elegance." Characters display their manners in the way they initiate or respond to conversation, in men's willingness to ask the ladies to dance so that no woman goes without a partner at a ball, in the effort a person shows in making visits and fulfilling social obligations, in conduct that controls anger and irritability in the presence of unpleasant company and exemplifies patience and forbearance, and in kind acts of thoughtfulness and pleasing that Austen calls "delicacy toward the feelings of others." Austen identifies the characters of good manners with the virtues of "amiability," "self-command," and "elegance." In short, propriety dictates that persons exert a conscious effort to make good first impressions and not only be good privately but also *appear* to be good publically so that outward conduct expresses good taste and that bad manners do not spoil the harmony of a social gathering.

If a person acts unsociable like Mr. Darcy at the Netherfield Ball and refuses to converse or dance, his manners impress no one, and he spoils the pleasantness of the event by his boorishness. Naturally no one seeks his friendship or expresses any desire to develop any relationship with him. Although Darcy is well bred and sophisticated, his manners were not "inviting," and Mrs. Bennet judges him "a most disagreeable, horrid man" for his lack of social graces: "Mrs. Long told me last night that he sat close to her for half an hour without once opening his lips." Darcy's breach of manners offends all the women at the assembly and stifles all chance of familiarity, friendship, or romance. On the other hand, Mr. Bingley wins approval and admiration, dancing with all the ladies and engaging in lighthearted, agreeable conversation. Jane pays him this compliment: " 'He was just what a young man ought to be,'" said she, " 'sensible, good humoured, lively; and I never saw such happy manners!—so much ease, with such perfect good breeding!'" In *Emma* Harriet Smith experiences great embarrassment at a ball because the snobbish Mr. Elton, the one eligible partner, will not deign to ask her to dance as he judges her beneath his notice and social class—an offense that Mr. Knightley and Emma condemn as "unpardonable rudeness." Noticing Harriet's awkwardness and humiliation at being slighted, Mr. Knightley chivalrously intervenes, winning Emma's admiration for this thoughtful gesture toward her friend: "Mr. Knightley leading Harriet to the set! . . . She was all pleasure and gratitude, both for Harriet and for herself, and longed to be thanking him." Darcy's arrogant manners at the ball frustrate all possibility of romance between him and Elizabeth even though he soon finds Elizabeth's eyes "bewitching" and feels attraction. On the other hand, Bingley's agreeable manners interest and please Jane, leading naturally to the beginnings of romance, and Emma's gratitude for Knightley's graciousness hints of her attraction to him.

In Austen's works a person expresses good manners by paying social calls and visiting neighbors and relatives, a skill that requires a sense of duty in honoring and pleasing others and demonstrates the virtues of patience and forbearance in the company of disagreeable people. In *Emma* several characters reveal thoughtless, immature conduct by their neglect of this social obligation. John Knightley, Knightley's brother who is married to Emma's sister, constantly complains about this custom of regular visits: "He anticipated nothing in the visit that could be at all worth the purchase; and the whole of their drive to the Vicarage was spent by him in expressing his discontent." He bemoans the fact of passing "five dull hours in another man's house, with nothing to say or to hear that was not said and heard yesterday, and may not be said and heard again to-morrow." Frank Churchill has failed to pay his respects to his widowed father who has recently married Miss Taylor. Constantly arranging for a visit and then reneging on his promise and always inventing far-fetched excuses like his obligations to honor the wishes of beloved relatives who cared for and educated him, Frank invites the criticism of both Emma and Mr. Knightley for his failure to be considerate of the feelings of his step-mother and of his debt to his father. Emma remarks, "[B]ut one cannot comprehend a young *man's* being under such restraint, as not to be able to spend a week with his father, if he likes it." Mr. Knightley's censure is more harsh: "There is one thing, Emma, which a man can always do, if he chuses, and that is, his duty; not by manoevering and finessing, but by vigour and resolution. It is Frank Churchill's duty to pay this attention to his father." In Knightley's judgment Frank lets expediency, pleasure, whim, and convenience rule his decisions rather than "respect for right conduct."

On the other hand, Mr. Knightley always fulfills his social obligations by inviting his brother's family to his home, coming to the Woodhouse home on a regular basis, and reprimanding Emma for her own failure to be kind toward the elderly Mrs. Bates and the garrulous Miss Bates whose company Emma finds tedious. Even though Mrs. and Miss Bates feel complimented by visits that bring great pleasure to their uneventful lives, Emma, like Frank, will not expend the effort because she finds the experience "very disagreeable,—a waste of time—tiresome women—and the horror of being in danger of falling in with the second rate and third rate of Highbury." This unsociable attitude of avoiding visits and inventing excuses resembles Darcy's snobbishness in refusing to dance or converse at the Meryton assembly. Bad manners, a manifestation of sloth, do not promote harmonious social life, and without pleasant sociable occasions the possibility of friendship, courtship, and romance diminish.

Social propriety also dictates that all persons govern their moods, emotions, and passions in the presence of company in public situations. Rather than make oneself the center of attention or the object of pity, good manners requires the "self-command" of reason rather than outbursts of sensibility. In *Sense and Sensibility* Austen portrays two sisters who suffer heart-breaking disappointments in love as their suitors, giving every impression of courtship and proposing marriage, abruptly end their romances and dash the hopes of the young women. Elinor, the older sister, discovers that her suitor Edward Ferrars has already been engaged privately, and Marianne, the younger daughter, finds herself jilted by Willoughby who has captured her heart and given everyone the impression of a chivalrous gentleman. While both sisters suffer the same sadness, Elinor never burdens others with her sorrows or spoils the mood of domestic tranquility or social mirth by displaying her feelings.

On the other hand, Marianne lies in bed in uncontrollable tears bemoaning her fate in a demonstration of self-pity at the home of Mrs. Jennings: "'Oh! Elinor, I am miserable indeed,' before her voice was entirely lost in sobs"—a condition exacerbated by her lack of sleep and appetite. When Elinor pleads, "Exert yourself, dear Marianne . . . if you would not kill yourself and all who love you. Think of your mother; think of all her misery while you suffer; for her sake you must exert yourself," Marianne reacts with utter helplessness: "'I cannot, I cannot,' cried Marianne; leave me, leave me if I distress; leave me, hate me, forget me!'" Venting all her unchecked emotions as if her grief alone deserves the foremost commiseration, Marianne occupies the center of attention and ignores the disturbance she causes and the suffering she places on others by her lack of restraint. This virtue of "self command" is the essence of civility which always respects the propriety of the occasion and considers the general happiness of others at the expense of indulging one's individual grief, anger, resentment, or moods. The desire to please others and never give offense or cause discomfort epitomizes the charity of civility that places others first and oneself last.

Good manners that promote social harmony and friendly relations with all people require magnanimity, the virtue of a large heart, soul, or mind that forgives the past, bears no grudges, and holds no petty grievances. This virtue of course opposes every form of small-mindedness like revenge, meanness, prejudice, and selfishness. None of the best romances or happiest marriages in Austen's novels grows without this generosity of the heart. In *Pride and Prejudice* Elizabeth's visit to Darcy's estate at Pemberley Woods with her aunt and uncle leads to an accidental encounter with Darcy who surprisingly returns home on business when the housekeeper assured the visitors of his absence. Because of Elizabeth's first impressions of Darcy's rudeness at the ball, his criticism of his friend Bingley's romance with Elizabeth's sister Jane, and his abrupt, premature condescending marriage proposal to Elizabeth without any form of proper courtship or effort to prove his worthiness, Elizabeth angrily rejected Darcy's first offer of marriage and acted most offended: "You could not have made me the offer of your hand in any possible way that would have tempted me to accept it," adding, "I had not known you a month before I felt that you were the last man in the world whom I could ever be prevailed on to marry."

Even though Darcy and Elizabeth's awkward meeting at Pemberley Woods recalls this unpleasant scene, neither one behaves with resentment or bitterness toward the other. Instead of acting cold and aloof toward the woman who insultingly rejected his offer of marriage, Darcy acts like a magnanimous gentleman and initiates cordial conversation, asks to be introduced to Elizabeth's aunt and uncle, and acts as a gracious host welcoming his guests: "That he should even speak to her was amazing!—but to speak with such civility, to enquire after her family! Never in her life had she seen his manners so little dignified, never had he spoken with such gentleness, as on this unexpected meeting." Elizabeth also acts with magnanimity, overlooking his earlier critical remarks about the bad manners of Mrs. Bennet and the younger Bennet sisters and forgiving his role in discouraging Bingley's match with Jane. Instead of behaving in a small-minded, unforgiving, vindictive way, both Darcy and Elizabeth are noble enough to admit their faults—his pride and her prejudice—and begin their relationship on the basis of good manners, this time "first impressions" that attract them to each other for good reasons.

A final aspect of manners that promotes sociability and harmony in mixed company is the famous principle of "well-regulated hatred" attributed to Austen. Sociability requires patience and tolerance for disagreeable people who violate the canons of propriety by poor taste and tactless behavior. No one should avoid social events because one person talks too much, another person never converses, and someone else's company is tiresome. Mrs. Bennet, described as "a woman of mean understanding, little information, and uncertain temper," says too much in public that should remain private and talks only of one subject, her daughters' prospects of marriage. Lydia Bennet offends by impertinence and unwelcome familiarity, lacks discretion by talking without thinking and always intruding on conversations. Lady Catherine in *Pride and Prejudice* and Mrs. Elton in *Emma* dominate conversations, Lady Catherine "dictating" her opinions to others and demanding information by "the impertinence of her questions" and Mrs. Elton, "well satisfied with herself, and thinking much of her own importance . . . meant to shine and be very superior." Mrs. Bates' stream of conversation has no beginning or end, and Mr. Woodhouse can only talk about the same subjects of health and weather. Frank Willoughby and Marianne spend all of their time together in private conversation and never mingle with company, and Jane Fairfax in *Emma* is too reserved and lacks the open temper Mr. Knightley admires in Emma. If Darcy and Bingley marry the Bennet sisters, they must accept and tolerate Mrs. Bennet's and Lydia's behavior without approving it. While Elizabeth is dining at Lady Catherine's home and subjected to her "delivering her opinion on every subject in so decisive a manner as proved she was not used to have her judgment controverted," Elizabeth demonstrates the principle of well-regulated hatred to maintain civility. No matter how arrogant Lady Catherine's manners or how officious her behavior, "Elizabeth felt all the impertinence of her questions, but answered them very composedly." One does not have to like every person at social occasions, enjoy their conversation, or approve of their manners, but it is a duty to promote amity and be at peace with everyone to foster harmony for the sake of everyone else's enjoyment. Even though Elizabeth disapproves of Mr. Wickham's elopement with Lydia and his lies about Darcy, once Wickham becomes her brother-in-law Elizabeth learns the importance of well-regulated hatred for the sake of family unity: "Come, Mr. Wickham, we are brother and sister, you know. Do not let us quarrel about the past."

Happy marriages, then, which offer "all the best blessings of existence," require courtships that allow love to grow and mature so that marriages offer more than economic security or social respectability to old maids and proper status to gentlemen.

The best marriages in Austen's novels—the matches of Darcy and Elizabeth, Knightley and Emma, Elinor and Edward Ferrars, and Marianne and Colonel Brandon— all follow a prelude of courtship in which the couples in the course of time know one another's mind and heart and appreciate the worthiness of the ones they respect and esteem.

These courtships do not result from the dictates of other family members like Mrs. Bennet or Lady Catherine or from the clever manipulation of matchmakers like Emma. Rather they develop naturally from introductions at social occasions and from long familiarity through friends and relatives who initiate social events that encourage the meeting of eligible men and women. During these assemblies, visits, and dinners the role of manners plays a major part in the course of true love. Without the desire to please by conversing with company and asking the ladies to dance, without the effort of performing the duty of visiting and making social calls, without the discipline of self command and the principle of well-regulated hatred, and without the habit of magnanimity by forgetting the past and forgiving the shortcomings of others, no social life is possible as the setting for romances to begin.

Happy marriages, then, can be traced to a person's good manners. Jane and Bingley's match can be traced to his gentleman's conduct at the ball. Elizabeth accepted Darcy's second proposal because his manners changed at Pemberley Woods from snobbish aristocrat to gallant knight. Knightley proposes to Emma when her manners improve—when she learns to stop her matchmaking and learns the graciousness of visiting company she finds dull. Elinor's magnanimity forgives Edward's lukewarm courtship because he apologizes for his youthful folly of an earlier engagement with Lucy Steele. And Marianne accepts the hand of Colonel Brandon because of his loyal affection and unwavering love during the entire time she and Willoughby were acting as if engaged. Through the art of courtship men express the wish of procuring a woman's "regard" and women become desirous of winning a man's "esteem"—the foundation for happy marriages in Jane Austen's England and for all ages.

Chapter 20. Anti-Life Ideology and the Reality of the "The Normal" in C.S. Lewis' *That Hideous Strength*

In C. S. Lewis's *That Hideous Strength* Mark Studdock, a young aspiring scholar seeking to distinguish himself in elite intellectual circles, feels flattered when the progressive, enlightened members of the National Institute for Coordinated Experiments (N.I.C.E.) offer him a position at Belbury. He is most thrilled when he receives the compliment of being addressed as "we". Formerly affiliated with the college at Edgestow and an outsider "watching the proceedings of what he then called 'Curry and his gang' with awe and with little understanding," Studdock feels great accomplishment at his promotion from outsider to member of the inner circle of the Progressive Element. With no knowledge of the Institute's agenda to apply scientific methods to all social problems ("the scientific reconstruction of the human race in the direction of increased efficiency"), Mark curries favor with the senior members of N.I.C.E. by championing the cause of "the preservation of the human race" to prove his unwavering allegiance to the cause of scientific progress. As he gradually gains more familiar knowledge of the organization's eugenics ideology—"sterilization of the unfit, liquidation of backward races (we don't want any dead weights), selective breeding"—Studdock makes no protests and has no reservations about his commitment to the cause of social advancement. He regards an affiliation with N.I.C.E. as a mark of the highest distinction: "And he, Mark, was to be in it all." He has no idea of the organization's diabolical anti-life, anti-nature, anti-human, anti-marriage ideology.

After his initiation into the Institute, Mark constantly wonders about the exact nature of his work and his particular responsibilities, only to receive vague answers and equivocations. The Deputy Director reassures Mark of the organization's admiration and appreciation of his abilities, welcomes him into "a very happy family" of colleagues, and explains that Mark's position is undefined and open ended: ". . . nobody wants to force you into any kind of waistcoat or bed of Procrustes. We do not really think, among ourselves, in terms of strictly demarcated functions, of course." All these evasions eventually convince Mark not to ask such questions lest he give the impression of bad manners or utter a "crudity." While Mark at first basks in the company of the elite, he soon wavers and considers changing his mind about joining N.I.C.E., especially as he becomes more acquainted with the strange nature of its members (an Italian eunuch, a mad parson, and a cigar smoking Miss Hardcastle) and their hidden agenda, their crusade to reinvent humanity "to something else, something better than human society." As Mark spends more time at the Institute and less time at home with his wife Jane, his zeal for N.I.C.E. slowly turns to revulsion, and the thought of leaving enters his mind more frequently: "But not at once. It would only be sensible to hang on for a bit and see how things shaped." Because Mark has been indoctrinated in his "modern" education with relativism, he holds no strong convictions or religious ideals—a defect that makes him an ideal candidate to advance the organization's agenda: ". . . in Mark's mind hardly one rag of noble thought, either Christian or pagan, had a secure lodging."

The secretive, elusive nature of the Institute begins to torment Mark to the point that he gives an ultimatum: either know his exact job description or leave the organization. When he protests, "But anything is better than being nominally in and having nothing to do," the answer he receives is, "The great thing is to do what you're told," that is, to be the unquestioning servant of N.I.C.E.—an assignment that ultimately develops into the role of the Institute's chief propagandist. Mark has been courted as a journalist to present the cause of N.I.C.E. in the most benevolent light. He is commissioned to report political, subversive events incited by the Institute before they even occur to predetermine public opinion. Despite Mark's dillusionment, the thought of becoming an outsider to an exclusive inner circle and the fear of a loss of salary influence him to stay. Indecisive and wavering, he at best can only resolve, "I have almost made up my mind not to take a full time job with N.I.C.E.," but then he adds, "But the D.D. [Deputy Director] won't hear of my leaving." The members of the inner circle forewarn Mark that "No one goes out of N.I.C.E." and "never to quarrel with anyone" and "It's not lucky to leave the N.I.C.E." Even after Mark finally learns that the Institute plans to use his talents as a propagandist and protests, "I'm not a journalist. I didn't come here to write newspaper articles," he never takes decisive action or resigns his position.

Imagining that he can assume the posture of neutrality and proceed by compromise, Mark finds it impossible to maintain the delicate balance between advancing in his career and honoring his marriage to Jane whom he rarely sees as N.I.C.E. pre-empts more of his time and talents. Repelled by the agenda of N.I.C.E. which Jane foresees in her dreams—a dead criminal's bodiless head restored to life by tubes and chemicals without the body as "the new man," she seeks relief in the company of simple, old-fashioned, family-loving people at St. Anne's who sense the horror of the experimentation, social engineering, and cultural revolution that N.I.C.E. is plotting. While at St. Anne's, Jane learns from one of the wise women, Camilla, that neither she nor Mark can be compromising or tolerant in the midst of this cultural war between the forces of N.I.C.E. planning to supplant Mother Nature and God the Father with the new scientifically engineered world that purports to eliminate all organic life and replace it with a modernized, improved version that invents artificial trees and bodiless men with mere heads to create a brave new utopian world in which "The human race is to become all Technocracy" and science makes men gods.

The metal tree—"no leaves in fall, no twigs, no birds building nests, no muck and no mess" and "no feathers dropped about, no nests, no eggs, no dirt"—hints of the Institute's ultimate goal of abolishing all organic life with its cycle of birth, growth, decay, and death. "The impure and the organic are interchangeable conceptions," Professor Filostrato explains. He loathes Mother Nature's processes—"all sprouting and budding and breeding and decaying"—as ungovernable, extravagant forces that accumulate filth and produce waste. Mother Nature's lavish fertility needs the taming of man's control so that stallions and bulls will be replaced by geldings and oxen. "There never will be peace and order and discipline so long as there is sex. When man has thrown it away, then he will become fully governable," Filostrato continues. The neutered, sexless, bodiless man of science will then allow for N.I.C.E.'s eugenics policy of population control and the elimination of retrogressive types classified as "unfit."

As a modern married couple Mark and Jane Studdock have placed their careers above their marriage and have alienated themselves from nature. Because Jane anticipates completion of her doctorate degree and foresees a future in scholarship after her marriage, "that was one of the reasons why they were to have no children, at any rate for a long time yet." As a married couple they live separate lives with only minimal contact, Mark preoccupied with his future ambitions at the Institute where he spends long days and late nights and Jane spending time at St. Anne's to compensate for her loneliness and to find relief from her nightmares about a headless man. Disappointed and frustrated, Jane does not feel that either she or Mark is in love: "Even when he was at home he hardly talked . . . why had he married her? Was he still in love?" N.I.C.E., then, not only glamorizes metal trees and bodiless men and decries the prodigality of Nature's fruitfulness but also holds marriage in contempt in the subtle ways it alienates Mark from his wife and exalts scientific progress above human love. Mark and Jane's modern education has divorced them from the normal, the human, and the natural to the degree that the cerebral abstractions of the Institute have greater reality to Mark than the physicality of his marriage to his wife. Mark's modern education "had the curious effect of making things that he read and wrote more real to him than the things he saw," and he developed the habit of never using words "man" or "woman" but instead terms like "vocational groups."

This situation of lukewarm neutrality in Mark and Jane's relationship—their insensibility to beauty, love, and marriage—cannot continue indefinitely without dehumanizing them. Therefore, Camilla, one of the members of St. Anne's, urges Jane to make a commitment rather than waver in indecision: "But don't you see . . . that you can't be neutral. If you don't give yourself to us, the enemy will use you." N.I.C.E. has urged Mark to persuade Jane to join the Institute because they wish to exploit her prophetic dreams. Denniston compares Jane's choice between good and evil to a daring deed, "a leap in the dark" that resembles the romance and adventure of heroes: "it is like that . . . like getting married, or going into the navy as a boy, or becoming a monk, or trying a new thing to eat. You can't know what it's like until you take the plunge." The members of St. Anne's waken Jane from her slumber of moral relativism and apathy by identifying the diabolical agenda of N.I.C.E. that threatens the whole human race. While St. Anne's stirs Jane's humanity and awakens her conscience, Mark undergoes a similar experience in which he too finally makes a commitment that leads him out of the mazes of the inner circles with their wheels within wheels that restores him to moral sanity and self-knowledge.

Because Mark's membership in the Institute becomes problematic because of his marriage and because of the secretive society and the duplicity of N.I.C.E. that trouble him, he soon feels threatened and fears for his life. He is put into a cell designed to condition him to think like all the other members of the inner circle. In this bizarre room Mark undergoes "a systematic training in objectivity" to dull the natural responses and normal reactions of human nature to good and evil, beautiful and ugly, normal and abnormal. Frost explains, "It is like killing a nerve. That whole system of instinctive preferences, whatever ethical, aesthetic, or logical disguise they wear, is to be simply destroyed." The oddly proportioned "objective room"—extremely high and too narrow—gives Mark a sense of an optical illusion because the point of the arch appears slightly off center and forces the observer to twist the head to see the correct position. Spots on the ceiling have the same effect of being irregularly arranged to resemble some approximate normal order just slightly skewed. A pattern on the table seems to duplicate the design on the ceiling, except that it is in reverse. When Mark beholds the art in the room, he sees a man with corkscrew arms, an open mouth with hair growing inside, a praying mantis playing a fiddle, and a swarm of beetles under the table at The Last Supper. Mark grasps the psychological indoctrination that he is undergoing—the aim of eliminating what Frost calls "that preposterous idea of an external standard," a form of conditioning "whereby all specifically human reactions were killed in a man" to fit him for evil.

While Frost naturally expects success from this psychological technique of desensitizing and dehumanizing man's stock responses to cultivate a taste for the perverse, the twisted, and the unnatural, Mark instead has the opposite reaction. The whole experiment illuminates for him the reality of the Natural: "As the desert first teaches men to love water, or as absence first reveals affection, there rose up against this background of the sour and the crooked some kind of vision of the sweet and the straight. Something else—something he vaguely called the 'Normal' apparently existed." The compromising, wavering, lukewarm intellectual deformed by a modern education in relativism suddenly experiences conviction and passion. Without any second thoughts or reservations Mark discovers the reality of the true, the good, and the beautiful that instantly come to mind when he thinks of Jane, fried eggs, sunlight, and the rooks that he misses desperately as the prisoner of N.I.C.E. Just as Jane finally committed to St. Anne's and took the plunge that resembled the finality of marriage, Mark also has drawn the battle line: "He was choosing a side: the Normal." If that position conflicted with the scientific point of view, "then be damned to the scientific point of view!"

The incarnate nature of goodness, beauty, and truth that Mark ultimately discovers in "the objective room" by its absence, Jane herself comes to know in the presence of cheerful people, happy marriages, innocent laughter, beautiful rooms, and the love of flowers and animals she finds at St. Anne's. Jane's false image of herself as an eminent scholar or as a childless married woman devoted to career surrenders to a new image of herself as woman, wife, and mother that is vibrant with Nature's vitality:" . . . the little idea of herself which she had hitherto called *me* dropped down and vanished . . . like a bird in a space without air. The name *me* was the name of a being whose existence she had never suspected . . . a made thing, made to please Another and in Him to please all others. . . ." In the atmosphere of ordinary people delighting in the simple pleasures of family living and loving relationships, Jane awakens into a new being who experiences a surge of life and joy and senses the reality of God in the glory of creation. This joy of life Jane sees when the elderly at St. Anne's dance, and "It seemed to each that the room was filled with kings and queens, that the wildness of their dance expressed their heroic energy and its quieter movements had seized the very spirit behind all noble ceremonies." In this company of the warm humanity at St. Anne's, Jane sees in the elderly not old age but a ripeness she compares to the fields of August in their radiant splendor, "serene and golden with the tranquility of fulfilled desire."

While Jane recovers her lost humanity and the joy of her femininity, Mark also reconsiders religion during the period of his indoctrination in the "objective room." Despite classifying Christianity as myth and superstition, Mark objects to Professor Frost's command to step on a cross to desecrate it, questioning why he needs to stamp on a face when Christianity has nothing to do with the scientist's idea of objectivity that Frost holds: "I mean . . . if it's only a piece of wood, why do anything about it?" If Frost and all of N.I.C.E. hold nothing but contempt for religion, why is Frost so adamant about directly assaulting something so nebulous as to be beneath their notice? Why were so many of the perverse pictures surrounding him attacks on religion? Why is N.I.C.E. making an enemy of nothing "objective"? As Mark ponders the symbolism of the crucifix and the image of the tortured, nailed body, another moment of illumination fills his mind similar to his discovery of the Normal: "It was a picture of what happened when the Straight met the Crooked, a picture of what the Crooked did to the Straight." Mark grasps the stark reality of evil as the perversion of the good and the natural. The neutral intellectual for whom good and evil were equivocal terms and mere abstractions with no real meaning or difference now apprehends the beauty of the Normal and the Straight with utter clarity and recognizes the ugliness of evil in all its loathsomeness.

Just as Mark eventually recognized that the mind's design for truth is as normal as the body's desire for water in a desert, he also accepts the reality that "his sensual desires were the true index of something which he lacked and Jane had to give." The created world has a meaning, purpose, and plan that no advanced institute for research should violate in the name of progress or experimentation. When Jane accompanies Mother Dimble to prepare the Lodge for the Maggs family, airing the rooms, adorning the house with flowers, and adding feminine touches of elegance, the older woman converses with the young bride about the comical side of marriage, reminding Jane that women who complain of men need to remember that they too have their crotchets: "And it isn't as if they hadn't a lot to put up with too . . . . whatever we say, Jane, a woman takes a lot of living with." When Jane voices the complaint that her husband hardly listens to her conversation, Mother Dimble quips, "Did it ever enter into your mind to ask whether anyone *could* listen to all we say?" Mother Dimble confesses that she herself cannot remember all she says when asked to repeat her words. Jane, then, acquires a fresh view of marriage as full of laughter, jokes, and frolics symbolized by the fairies that attend bridal bowers and marriage beds. Little does Jane know that the Lodge she is preparing for the Maggs family will be her own chamber when she and Mark are finally reunited by the knowledge of their love and the truth of their humanity.

Longing for one another after their long separation, Mark no longer values his association with elite organizations as his supreme priority in life, and Jane no longer equates her identity with her ambitions for a career in academe. As she walks to the Lodge with the anticipation of Mark's arrival before her, she sees only darkness and a closed door, fearing that Mark had lost interest in her and worrying "what if Mark did not want her—not tonight, nor in that way, nor any time, nor in any way?" But when she notices the opening of the bedroom window and clothes carelessly thrown on a chair, she no longer hesitates: "Obviously it was high time she went in." Mark and Jane, then, return to the Normal, rediscover the Natural, and marvel at the goodness of the incarnate world. No Progressive Elements in academe, no efficient scientifically engineered world without organic life, and no invented bodiless men offer what Mother Nature and God the Father give in the fullness of life and love symbolized by the union of man and woman in the flesh.

God's good creation and Mother Nature's prodigality give Mark and Jane what no sterile, clean, efficient, reinvented "new man" can imitate or improve—the reality of the masculine and the feminine. Jane finally understands the great lesson St. Anne's tries to teach her: "You are offended by the masculine itself: the loud, irruptive, possessive thing—the gold lion, the bearded bull—which breaks through hedges and scatters the little kingdom of your primness as the dwarfs scattered the carefully made bed."

Additional Reading

Siobhan Nash-Marshall
Joan of Arc
A Spiritual Biography

Written in a straight-forward, concise, and at times humorous manner, Nash-Marshall's Joan of Arc acquaints the reader with a historical character who became a legend during her lifetime legend. Joan is presented to us as a brave young girl who received a mission and who courageously used all of her faculties and gifts to accomplish it. Nash Marshall's approach is refreshingly honest. The narrative is centered on Joan, her mission, her work to fulfill it, her betrayal. The author gives us the facts and allows us readers to draw our own conclusions. Lovers of history will find the author's thesis on the connection between the resurgence of France, the betrayal of Joan, and the fall of Byzantium very interesting.

978-0-8245-9905-8/pb/192 pages

Support your local bookstore or order
directly from the publisher at www.crossroadpublishing.com

To request a catalog or inquire about
Quantity orders, e-mail
sales@crossroadpublishing.com

The Crossroad Publishing Company